Diamonds

Diamonds in the Rough

Heartfelt, Spiritual Poems for Those That are Grieving
A Tribute to My Son, Travis

I am an Angel Mom

Don't judge my path if you have not walked my journey

Donna Carpenter

Diamonds in the Rough

Donna Carpenter

Diamonds in the Rough

Copyright © 2021 written by Donna Carpenter.

Copyright © 2021 published by LSW Media Group

All rights reserved.

No part of this publication may be reproduced, stored in a retrieval system or transmitted in any way by any means, electronic, mechanical, photocopy, recording or otherwise without the prior permission of the author except as provided by USA copyright law.

The opinions expressed by the author are not necessarily those of LSW Media Group.

Published by: LSW Media Group

Charlotte, NC 28210
Phone: 704-649-6358
Please Email Manuscripts to: publish@lswmediagroup.com

Authored by Donna Carpenter
Book design copyright © 2021 by Cyndilu Miller. All rights reserved.
Cover Design by: Cyndilu Miller. All rights reserved.
Layout by LSW Media Group
Editor: LSW Media Group

Published in the United States of America

ISBN: 9798531178206

Date: July 1, 2021

Diamonds in the Rough

Diamonds in the Rough

Heartfelt, Spiritual Poems for Those That are Grieving
A Tribute to My Son, Travis

Diamonds in the Rough

Diamonds in the Rough

DEDICATION

First and foremost, I would like to thank the Lord for His part in leading me and giving me the words to my poems. Without Him, I couldn't have written them like they are.

I have poured my heart and soul into these poems in hopes of bringing comfort to other grieving families. While writing some of them I had tears running down my face.

I feel like the words I write do help me in my grief in the loss of my son, Travis.

I want to thank an awesome lady, Jacqueline Smith for her part in getting this book published. She came to me and said that God had called on her to assist me in publishing this book, I can't thank her enough.

Diamonds in the Rough

I would like to thank another sweet lady for doing the artwork on this book, Cyndilu Miller, you did an awesome job with the graphics on the cover.

I'd like to thank my daughter, Lindsay, for encouraging me to get my poems together and get them published.

I want to dedicate this book to my husband, Mark who passed on June 10, 2010 and my son, Travis who passed on April 6, 2019.

Diamonds in the Rough

Contents

God Holds Me In His Hands	21
I Told Him Goodbye	22
Keeping the Faith	23
Peace and Joy He's Brought	25
Your Cherry Blossom Tree	26
It's Raining On The Inside	27
Forever They'll Stay	28
Heaven Doesn't Seem So Far	29
To Bring You Comfort	30
If You Only Knew	32
My Heart Will Go On	33
My Special Boy	34
I'll See You Son, One Day	35
Someday We Might Heal	36
A Window To Heaven	37
A Gift To Me	38
A Dream Of You	39
Would You?	40
In Heaven Among The Stars	41
I'll Praise Him Through Life's Storms	42
Finally Set Free	44
God's Here, Twenty-Four, Seven	46
I Am Stronger	47
I'll Let Go	48

Diamonds in the Rough

This Storm	49
If I Had One Wish	50
Pain We've Never Felt	51
God's Promise To Us	53
By Your Side, He'll Stay	54
Reminiscing	55
Each Day Brings Me Closer	56
My Son's Glorious Home	57
A Life Of Splendor	58
I'm Thinking Back	59
God Gives Me His Strength	60
His Precious Face I'll See	61
Peace And Joy We'll Find	63
If I Could Reach To Heaven	64
Experiencing Heaven	65
God's In Control	66
I Decided	67
Real Peace I Will Find	68
God Has Kept Me Strong	69
Seeing Him Face To Face	70
God Whispered His Name	71
His Shining Light	72
A Place I Long To Go	73
You're In Paradise	75
Peace Of Mind	76

Diamonds in the Rough

God Knew What Was Best For You	77
I Wonder	78
My Funny Boy	80
You're Finally Happy Where You Are	82
He's In My Heart	83
My Gift God's Given Me	84
I'll See You In A Different Light	85
Only The Lord Knows	86
Our Faith	87
We'll Forever Stay	89
I'll Cherish The Memories	90
I'm Trying To Imagine	91
I'll See You Soon	92
A Window To Heaven	93
In Heaven, Up On High	94
I'll Be There In A While	95
What A Reunion	96
You're Dear to God's Heart	98
God Is Never Late	99
God's Love Is The Best	100
He's in Heaven	102
His Dream	104
He's Resting In Jesus	106
Their Hearts Are Saddened	108
In the Presence Of God	109

Diamonds in the Rough

This Illness	110
I'll Embrace Them	111
Our Home In Heaven	112
He Has Made Me Strong	113
He Carries Me	115
Peace And Joy He's Brought	116
God Is Here	117
This Mountain	118
God Took His Pain Away	119
This Grief Won't Keep Me Down	120
Only the Lord Understands	121
Our Pain Is Everyday	122
I'll See Them Again	123
He'll Call Me Home	124
God's With Us To Stay	125
I'll See My Son Again	126
Our Children Are Peaceful	127
Looking Forward To Heaven	128
A Home In Heaven	129
Safely To The End	130
I Will Comfort You	131
God's Plans	132
A Glorious Day	133
I Long To See My Boy	135
You're Happy And Peaceful	136

Diamonds in the Rough

Forever More	137
We're Going To Make It	138
Our Hearts Will Mend	139
You're In Heaven Now	140
If You Knew	141
The Lord Knows	145
I'm In His Arms	146
I'll Meet Them At The Gate	147
If I Could Have One Wish	148
I'd Climb The Highest Mountain	149
Reunited We'll Be	151
Our Broken Hearts	153
In My Heart To Stay	154
The Dream	155
My Poems I Write	156
They're Healed By The Masters Touch	158
A Chance To Heal	159
With Me God Will Always Be	160
In My Heart He Stays	161
He Holds Me In His Arms	163
Good Times We Had	164
I Hold My Head High	165
We'll Get Through	166
I'll See You In A Little While	167
I Thought The World Of You	168

Diamonds in the Rough

All That Matters	169
For A Little While	171
I've Finally Made It Home	172
Releasing These Tears	173
You've Crossed Over	174
Your Dad And You	175
I Adored Our Time Together	176
God's Taking Care Of You	177
Dreams Of You	178
A Glorious Place	179
How Happy I Will Be	180
In Heaven Is Where I'll Be	182
I Want Him Here	184
Your Pain And Tears Are Erased	186
Someday I Will See	187
Our Broken Hearts Will Be Healed	189
A Brighter Tomorrow	190
I Hold You In My Heart	192
My Life Won't Fade	193
Your Beautiful Tree	194
I Hold Him Dear	195
Someday I Will Know	197
You're In My Heart	198
God Stays By My Side	199
Missing You	200

Diamonds in the Rough

It's Ok To Cry	201
Many People Are Hurting	202
Healed By His Touch	204
In His Hands	205
The Letter	206
In Perfect Peace	207
You're Happy	208
Tired And Weary	209
A Special Dream Of You	210
All That I Am	211
His Pain Will Cease	212
The Best Son Of All	213
You'll Know Him	214
Where The Skies Are Blue	215
He Makes Me Stronger	216
I'll See You, Again	217
God Has Been Good To Me	218
His Pain And Heartache Are Done	219
Words God's Given Me	220
Through Each Day	221
I'll Rise Above The Pain	222
My Dream Of You	224
My Heart May Heal	225
Fill Me With Your Peace	226
God Gives Me Strength	228

Diamonds in the Rough

You're On My Mind	230
You're Healed By The Master's Touch	231
My Precious Boy	232
Mesmerized	234
Can't Wait To See You	235
Grieving You	236
He Has Me In His Hands	238
Peaceful I Will Be	240
Nothing Has Prepared Me	241
Memories Of You	242
I'll Never Give Up	243
God Can Bring Us Peace	245
I'll See You Again	246
Since The Day You Were Born	247
A Place For Us In Heaven	249
The Lord Blesses Me	250
Mental Illness Is Horror	252
He's Been There For Me	254
God Sees Our Pain	256
God's Getting Me Through	257
We Know They're At Peace	258
I'm Busy Missing You	260
God's Presence	262
This Crippling Disease	263
If You Could Come Back	265

Diamonds in the Rough

The Lord Can Get Them Through	266
I'd Hold You Tight	267
Poems For You	268
What A Glorious Day	269
If I Could Visit Heaven	270
I'd Rather Have You In Heaven	271
These Waves Of Grief	273
My Memories Of Us	274
I Love You To The Moon	276
God's Bottling Up My Tears	277
God's Taken Your Pain Away	278
This Journey	280
The Job You Loved	281
Not In A Million Years	282
Pain From Loving You	283
If I Could Reach To Heaven	284
You'll Be In My Heart	285
To All The Mothers	287
Stormy Storms	289
Through My Tragedies	291
My Longing To Help Others	292
I Trust In Him	294
He Sets Me Free	295
Life's Trials And Tribulations	296
His Love For Me	297

Diamonds in the Rough

He'll Wipe My Tears Away 298
Heaven Bound 299
You'll Abide In Him 300
It Doesn't Feel Real 301
Grief So Painful 302
He's Bottling Up Our Tears 303
At Peace I'll Be 304
Our Grief Washed Away 306
Heaven Is Where They Belong 307
A Sign 308
We Need Compassion 309
You're On My Mind 310
Mother's Day 311
The Grief That Stays 312
A New Life 314
God Was There For You 315
I Have Hope 316
Poems For You 318
God Gave You Rest 319
I'll Hold You In Heaven 320
Sometimes I Just Breathe 322
God Answered Our Prayers 323
He Wiped Your Tears Away 325
His Strength 326
Peace He Brings Me 328

Diamonds in the Rough

A Better Place	329
The Very Best	331
I Miss My Husband	332
In A Better Place	333
God's Purpose For You	334
My Heart Is Sad	335
I Grieve For You	336
My Heart Will Mend	337
Mother's Day	338
I'll Keep You In My Heart	340
Remembering You	341
I'm Thinking About You	342
Thinking About You	344
There With Jesus	345
Heaven	347
He's Wiped Your Tears Away	348
Trust The Lord	349
Your Heart's Door	350
Heavenly Birthday	351
He's All You've Got	353
Refuge From The Storm	355
Promised Land	357
God's There	358
You're At Peace	359
A Special Grandson	360

Diamonds in the Rough

Can't Compare 361
A Journey 363
Save Me A Place 364
Don't Cry For Me 365
Always Strong 367
I've Moved Ahead 368
Don't Tell Me 369
You're Healed 370
I Want You Near 371
Never Ending Peace 372
Your Time To Go 374
At Home With Jesus 376
No Pain Or Tears 377
In The Promised Land 379
A Heavy Heart 380
Imagine Heaven 381
Hard Times 382
You Longed For Heaven 383
I'll See You, Son 384
Waves Of Pain 385
I Am Thankful 386
If You Could See Me 387
A Changed Life 389
You've Gone Before Me 391
Hard Roads 392

Diamonds in the Rough

A Smile Upon Your Face	393
I'll Take This Pain Away	394
No Pain In Heaven	395
Trusting You	396
Through The Storm	398
Many Moods	399
My Journey	400
Suicide	403
Jesus Suffered Too	405
If I Could	407
God Chose You	408
God's Plans	409
Someday I'll Know	410
I Taught You	411
Your Heavenly Birthday	412
My Home In Heaven	413
People Are Hurting	414
The Strength God Gives	415
You're At Peace	417
At Peace	418
God's Got My Back	421
Hard Times	422
He'll Give You Back To Me	424
I'll See You Again, Son	425
I Love You, Son	426

Diamonds in the Rough

I Said Goodbye	427
The Peace He Brings	428
Our Child	429
Enjoying Heaven	430
Trust God	431
I'll Move On	432
He's In A Better Place	433
Grief Is Love	434
I Miss You	435
Faith	436
I'll See You Again	438
He Set Me Free	439
A Broken Heart	440
This Illness	441
Your Hearts Door	442
Your Gift To Me	443
Because He Lives	444

Diamonds in the Rough

God Holds Me In His Hands

I know God holds me in His hands
And He resides in my heart
He helps me with my struggling
Because my child and I are apart!

I've turned my suffering soul over to Him
And given Him my whole heart
I know He's capable of healing me
I feel the love and peace He's brought!

My emotions come and go so much
And I'm definitely feeling the blow
Wondering how long it'll last
Pain from letting my precious son go!

I know he's in the arms of the Lord
There's nothing to worry about anymore
He's finally received such perfect peace
Like he never had before!

I know my heart will always be sad
When I think of my son each day
Sometimes it's so heavy with grief
I just go to God and pray!

I know people are suffering like me
They've lost a child or two
And I know they're traveling a road so hard
A journey that they never knew!

Diamonds in the Rough

I Told Him Goodbye

The anniversary of my son is coming up real soon
And I know there'll be tears in my eyes
Two years have gone by so fast
Two years since I told him goodbye!

I think that I'm trying to accept it
His death that's taken a toll on me
Such pain that I've never felt before
I don't want others to see

Most people don't know what to say
They change the subject real fast
They just don't know or understand
That this heartache for years could last

I really am tired of crying
And I hide it when I need to
Tears coming down like the rain
It's just something I need to do!

We think about our children all the time
And wonder how long it will be
Before we'll be reunited with them
What a sight we'll see!

Beautiful voices, halos of gold
Love and peacefulness everywhere
It really brings my heart joy
I just can't imagine being there!

Diamonds in the Rough

Keeping the Faith

I'm truly going to keep the faith
No matter what comes my way
I trust God like never before
To get me through each day!

He's lifted me up, set me on high
He has mighty plans for me
Even if I'm not aware of them
Even if His will, I can't see!

He hasn't brought me this far for nothing
And He hasn't forgotten the pain I've been through
He's been in my life every minute
Brought me some peace and understanding too!

Some ask how can I have assurance when I've been through so much
I tell them God's using my ashes to make beauty
I don't question Him like I've done before
Someday His will, I'll see

God knows what we never will
Not in this life, not here
He's looking down on us wounded
And bottling up all our tears

Diamonds in the Rough

God will answer us in His time
Patient we just need to be
He's the one my heart counts on
Peace and joy He'll bring to me!

Diamonds in the Rough

Peace and Joy He's Brought

The Lord doesn't promise a life without pain
The sun won't shine everyday
There will be days of darkness
Sometimes you'll feel it will stay!

Whether you believe in a sovereign God
He still loves you anyway
When He whispers in a gentle voice
He wants you to open up and pray

I've prayed more in this last year
Than I ever have before
Thinking of my son that's gone
Of my baby boy that I bore!

God doesn't expect me to understand
Why my boy had to go
I just feel like my heart is broken
And I just loved him so!

Time could take some of the pain away
That I've heard before
I know God has a plan for me
I long to know what He has in store!

I've accepted what has happened
Although this grief has broken my heart
God promises to get me through
Some peace and joy He has brought!

Diamonds in the Rough

Your Cherry Blossom Tree

Down beneath the garden
Sits your cherry blossom tree
I planted it just for you
To bring some joy to me!

I ask the Lord to let it grow
Strong for many years
I go to visit often
And my eyes fill up with tears!

I've placed a few things there for you
All around that blossom tree
Just filling it up with things you liked
A really nice site to see!

First, there's a small amount of your ashes
Placed down under the ground
Then two statues of cats you loved
You just loved yours being around!

A flag with your picture there
Then a Angels beautiful wings
I know now in Heaven they surround you
And you listen to them as they sing!

I'll enjoy your tree for many years
As I visit I'll be thinking about you
Maybe someday this load will lighten
I so love and miss you too!

Diamonds in the Rough

It's Raining On The Inside

It's raining on the inside of me
The tears are flooding my eyes
A mighty storm is brewing
All I can do is sit here and cry!

It hurts more than anything I've ever felt
For me to lose my precious son
And his dad just went before him
Sometimes I feel like I'm done!

For many years I took care of them
But my sons illness I couldn't touch
I just wished I could've had a miracle
Because I love and miss them so much!

The Lord knows how much I've prayed
To release this pain for awhile
I know bad things can happen
And often times we go through trials!

It feels there's a knife burning through my heart
How much more can I stand?
I know I'll never grieve for a moment
That God's not holding my hand!

This grief feels like it's been here too long
I'm feeling the agony of losing you
But I'm not one to give it up
Because surviving is what I do!

Diamonds in the Rough

Forever They'll Stay

You are trying your best to get by
Your child hasn't been gone that long
The pain inside seems to strangle you
You feel their death just seems so wrong!

You've been sitting in your room just crying
Not even counting the hours
Nothing is making any sense to you
Your life feels like it's just a blur!

Your child isn't in pain anymore
They're in Heaven, they've been set free
Free from all heartache and sorrow
And that's just amazing to me!

I know you're longing to see them again
Their absence has taken a piece of your heart
You're thinking of the years you had with them
And feeling the love they brought!

Through my own heartache and pain
I try to see it in a different way
Knowing I will see my son again
What a Glorious day!

Just know that they're at peace right now
God has wiped their tears away
What a magnificent place they're in
For Eternity, forever they'll stay!

Diamonds in the Rough

Heaven Doesn't Seem So Far

We walked down the path through the field
To pick a bunch of pretty flowers
After awhile a dark cloud came
So we ran fast through the spring showers!

I always enjoyed my time with you
It really put joy in my heart
You always knew that you were loved
And that love is what God brought!

You sang songs that I taught you
When you were just a few years old
I saved those tapes of you singing
You seemed happy down in your soul!

I wish I could have those sweet moments back
Just for a little while
I'm really missing you so much
Because you were my precious child!

I was sad alot of times
Because I knew what the future would hold for you
I watched you through your illness
And I knew what you would do!

As much as I miss you I'm still happy
Because I know where you are
Sometimes I feel you are here
And then Heaven doesn't seem to far!

Diamonds in the Rough

To Bring You Comfort

I'm sitting in the dark, daydreaming about you again
But this is nothing that's new
It's something that I do everyday
Because I love and miss you!

Most don't know the depth of my pain
And it's something no one should have to feel
Everyday that comes and goes
Your absence becomes more real!

Sometimes I'm afraid of what the future holds
Will I lose someone else again?
I don't know if I could deal with that
Because down that long road I've already been!

I don't think God is punishing me
Although sometimes it feels that way
But down in my heart I know it's not true
He's here with me everyday!

He sees my eyes that are swollen
And tears running down my face
And He knows sometimes I want to go home
To be in that Glorious place!

I don't know what the future holds for me
It's in my Fathers hands
But when I meet Him face to face
I'll finally understand!

Diamonds in the Rough

I'll know what the purpose was for my life
And the reason for the pain I've been through
Then I'll know that some of my pain
Was to bring some comfort to you!

Diamonds in the Rough

If You Only Knew

My heart just flutters, it skips a beat
When my mind is fixed on you
I know you didn't mean to hurt me
Oh son, if you only knew !

If you knew about the restless nights
When all I can do is cry
If you could look upon my face
You'd see the tears pouring from my eyes!

People think this grieving should be over
Sometimes I make excuses for myself
I wonder how they'd feel if their child was gone?
And there ashes were sitting on a shelf!

I'd never wish this on anyone
It is a nightmare in disguise
I wish people would be more sympathetic
Knowing we had to tell our child goodbye!

I think the worse part is missing them
After years and years go by
We realize that they're not here
And sometimes we ask God why?

I've never questioned the Lord about this tragedy
Because someday He'll let me know
But right now my mind is thinking about him
Because I love and miss him so!

Diamonds in the Rough

My Heart Will Go On

That night God called you home
Was the night He set you free
He knew you were in tremendous pain
So He took you where you needed to be!

I knew all along what you had planned
You had no business with a gun
I really wish you had of listened to me
But now the damage has been done!

Although you had God in your life
You still struggled with your illness so much
My heart and soul are crying out for you
I wish your face I could touch !

The Lord has given me the strength to ease my pain
But still it can get pretty tough
He comes and sits beside me
Because He knows that I've had enough!

I feel like this agony will someday let up
And I think that I will heal
But right now I'm trying to mend my heart
And what happened feels so real!

I've never felt bitter about this tragedy
Because I know that God's in control
And I know that He'll answer my questions someday
Everything then will unfold!

Diamonds in the Rough

My Special Boy

My son would throw snowballs at me in the winter
And pull me with his four-wheeler in the snow
We had so much fun together
I'll never let these memories go!

He was a good boy but so peculiar
I saw it from the start
I tried to help him get through it
Frustration and tears, it brought!

My son didn't make many friends
Because he was an introvert
He'd sit in his room for hours
And that made my heart really hurt!

He didn't invite friends for his birthday
He just wanted his family here
He seemed to be a loner for awhile
He struggled with anxiety and fear!

As he got older, it was worse
It was hard to know what to do
I tried to get him the help he needed
And I told him how much I loved him, too!

Now he's definitely in a better place
I know he has peace and joy
And I can't wait to greet him with open arms
He will always be my special boy!

Diamonds in the Rough

I'll See You Son, One Day

These waves I feel aren't crashing as hard
And sometimes I might even have an ok day
But when they come out of the blue
I just go to God and pray!

He's the one that gets me through
Every day as I morn
I just can't believe that this is real
That's the reason my heart is so torn!

My son I loved was everything
Such a precious boy
Sometimes I was mesmerized by him
Because he brought me alot of joy!

I'm just not ready to give him up
But that's not reality
I know in my heart that he's not here
Because the Lord has set him free!

If I could see him one more time
And see his beautiful smile
I'd so much want to be with him
Maybe it'll be in a little while!

I'm not saying that I'm ready to go
There are things I can't leave undone
I have some of my family here
But one day I'll be with my son!

Diamonds in the Rough

Someday We Might Heal

I don't know you grieving mothers
But I feel the pain you're going through
Last year I lost my precious child
And I know that you did too!

Where do we go from here?
With such a broken heart
Pain that never really stops
It just tears us all apart!

I thought time would make it better
Like others said it would do
But every time the tears run down
I know that it isn't true!

How can the pain just disappear?
When we're hurting so bad
We hope it will someday
But right now I'm so, so sad!

Friends of ours don't really know
The horror that we go through
Because we've lost our precious children
To them they have no clue!

I feel so sorry for all of us
Because our pain is real
It's a pain we feel every day
Maybe someday we will heal!

Diamonds in the Rough

A Window To Heaven

If I could look through a window and see Heaven
And see so much peacefulness there
If I could see the gates of pearl
And streets of gold everywhere!

I would see my son running toward me
And I would embrace him like never before
I would feel the love in his heart
And know that there's so much more!

I've known about a place called Heaven
I was taught many years ago
And I shared this with my son when he was little
I told him how God loves him so!

He's never forgot what I taught him
He talked alot about going there
I knew he was tired and weary
And tired of the pain he had to bear!

He didn't talk much about his illness
But I saw the pain in his eyes
I knew someday it would happen
That I would have to tell him goodbye!

That window to Heaven is closed again
But I'll see my son someday
And once again he'll come running to me
And I'll be there with him to stay!

Diamonds in the Rough

A Gift To Me

Your little boy came to visit me today
And boy, is he just like you!
I tried to hide the tears from him
Why I was crying, he already knew!

I don't want him to see me this way
Just down and feeling sad
I know he thinks about his dad at times
And the fun that they had!

Because of my son's illness
A father he didn't think he could be
He thought he had nothing to offer his boy
And this really troubled me!

At times I tried to reason with him
But he didn't seem to understand
My son never had any self-worth
But he was a caring, compassionate man!

I know my grandson misses me
The me I use to be
But I don't know if I'll ever get back
To be the same old me!

What a gift my son has left for me
Such a handsome, precious little boy
A child I'll always cherish
He has brought me so much joy!

Diamonds in the Rough

A Dream Of You

In the dream I had of you last night
I saw the happiness on your face
Your eyes were lit up so bright
Because Heaven is a magnificent place!

The dream has been on my mind all day
I feel such joy in my soul
I knew then that Heaven was so real
Just liked times that I'd been told!

What an awesome place to be right now
With God and Angels that sing
Living a life that's so perfect
And feeling the love God brings!

I saw you with all our family
The ones that have gone before me
Embracing each other with love in their heart
A place you'll be for Eternity !

Although I miss you so, so much
I need to concentrate on your happiness
There's no doubt in my mind
That you're in a place with Heavenly bliss!

One day this grief may not seem too bad
I can't wait until that day
And someday the Lord will take me home
He'll wipe my pain and tears away!

Diamonds in the Rough

Would You?

If you met me on the street one morning
And you felt I was having a bad day
Would you comfort me and see my tears
Or would you turn the other way?

Would you give me a chance to tell my story
Could you make enough time for me?
Although you're a stranger I'd do it for you
Please let me tell you about my hearts misery!

It would only take five or ten minutes
To tell you about my broken heart
I would tell you about how I lost my son
And now we have to be far apart!

Would you let me tell you about my life?
Or would it make any difference to you?
I would tell you how God made beauty from my ashes
And helping people is what I want to do!

Would you try to understand what I'm going through?
Even though you've probably haven't been through this
I would tell you that when I saw my son
It ended with goodbye and then a kiss!

If you don't want to be bothered, then please just go
Because I know there are people that care
And I know they will be there for me
And my pain they'll help me bear!

Diamonds in the Rough

In Heaven Among The Stars

I can't pretend that you're still here
Just gone away for awhile
Thinking I'm going to see you again
I miss you so much, my child!

I miss you far more than anyone else
These feelings I can't contain
Tears flowing down my face
Like a flood from the falling rain!

I just wish I could have known your pain
Maybe I could've figured it out
And gotten the help you needed
You would've gotten better, I don't have a doubt!

But you decided to do it your way
I know you had a lot on your mind
You just decided to stop your agony
And leave this world behind!

I haven't been angry at you for a minute
Because I know what you were going through
You heart was in much misery
I only wanted the best for you!

I try not to be sad about you every moment
Because I know where you are
There with the Lord and your dad
You're in Heaven among the stars!

Diamonds in the Rough

I'll Praise Him Through Life's Storms

I praise God in the good times of life
And I also praise Him in the bad
I don't blame Him for anything
Not for the life I've had!

Some people seem to sail smoothly through life
We say in their mouth they were born with a silver spoon
Everything always going their way
And they're often over the moon!

God is the only one that knows my heart
And He knows how much I can take
He's given me His strength through the years
When He knew my heart would break!

I'll never know why things happen like they do
And it's not for me to figure out
So many years I've put my trust in God
He's the one that knows what it's all about!

I know the Lord is using me
To go and get the job done
There are so many people hurting
Like me because I've lost my son!

God doesn't ask too much of us
He just wants to free our pain and give us joy
But I know it will take awhile for me
Because of the pain from losing my boy!

Diamonds in the Rough

I'll always praise God in the storms of life
Although I've had quite a few
He just ask me to trust Him
So that's what I'm going to do!

Diamonds in the Rough

Finally Set Free

Please don't do away with yourself
Just know that God really loves you
He sees your pain and heartache
And the illness in your mind too!

It's nothing to be ashamed of
Most of us were born that way
I've spent years and years struggling
It was each and everyday!

I've felt the way that you have
Suicidal thoughts in my mind
Just not knowing how to get better
Peace and happiness I was looking to find!

That peace and happiness didn't come right away
I fought like never before
Just wanting to have a normal life
Just thinking I couldn't take anymore!

I spent most of my life trying to survive
I felt my heart was going to break
After awhile when I didn't get better
Suicidal plans I was going to make!

I didn't know at the time God was watching over me
He stopped me from going through with my plan
I know now that He saved my life
All along, He had me in His hands!

Diamonds in the Rough

I ask God many times to heal me
And one day a few years ago, He came through
I've never suffered again with the pain and depression
And He can do the same for you!

Along with medicine and therapy
It took awhile to get it right
With the Lords help I worked real hard
And at the end of the tunnel was a light!

I knew that had been a breaking point
And at first I didn't see
But all along God was planning
To finally set me free!

Diamonds in the Rough

God's Here, Twenty-Four, Seven

There will come a time in the future
When I will realize where I've been
The pain and heartache of a lifetime
I pray that I will never have to live it again!

God is in my life and I feel Him
He gives me much needed strength to go on
He knows every fiber of my being
And He knew me before I was born!

Trials and tribulations come and go
And most times it leaves a broken heart
There's only one that I can turn to
Love and peacefulness God's brought!

He knows the burdens that I bear
And He sees my pain and tears
He longs to give me happiness and joy
To rid me of anxiety and fear!

It's almost impossible to explain to others
The pain and devastation that we feel
And when you lose a precious child
It will take a long time to heal!

I just can't brag enough for what God does
He's here for me, twenty-four, seven
As long as I'm here, He won't leave my side
And then He'll call me to my home in Heaven!

Diamonds in the Rough

I Am Stronger

I am stronger than I know
I am still here, I did not die
I leaned over and kissed his cheek
The day I told my son goodbye!

The hardest thing I've ever done
Was to see my son lying there
Just wanting to hold his lifeless body
While the tears fell everywhere!

This last year has been the hardest
Of all the years gone by
More pain that my heart has ever felt
But still, I will not die!

I will not take myself from this life
Even though the thought of Heaven feels good
I know there are people counting on me
I'll stay in this world like I should!

My daughter knows the pain I've had in this life
She says God is giving me too much
I said that He is by my side
And I'll be healed one day by just His touch!

The Lord knows how much I can handle
He sees the strength that He's given me
And He knows this heartache won't last
Because I'll be with Him through Eternity!

Diamonds in the Rough

I'll Let Go

Somedays this pain just grips me so tight
And other days I sail right through
But the waves often are monstrous
Because I'm grieving so hard for you!

I just can't believe you're not with me
You can't imagine what it's done to my heart
My heart that knows you're not coming back
And now we have to be apart!

Pain and tears like never before
Been crying for over a year
Somedays I push through it
I grieve other days because you're not here!

To me this tragedy is hard to accept
Even though some time has gone by
I know God had a purpose for it
So I've never even asked Him why?

You were so handsome and charming
And you always had a girl
My only son and I was proud of you
A beautiful addition to this world!

Maybe in the future, I can let go
Because I depend on the Lord to get me through
He knows the burden that's been on my heart
And He knows I love and miss you!

Diamonds in the Rough

This Storm

I've seen hurricanes and many storms
And my tears coming down like rain
I try to stay strong as I need to
But I feel at times I'm going insane!

Sometimes these storms, I can't control
And they carry me out to sea
Blinded by the capsizing waves
It really gets ahold of me!

The smaller storms I can handle
Because I've been through them before
I try to take each breath slowly
Sometimes it feels like a war!

The storm in my life now is raging
It's the worst I've ever been through
It tries to take control of me
Holding on is all I can do!

I beg the waves to lighten up
Don't know how much I can take
Although I'm doing better than I thought
I have to protect myself for my sake!

The heaviest storms will let up one day
And stronger my mind will be
My heart and soul will never forget
What this storm has done to me!

Diamonds in the Rough

If I Had One Wish

If God would grant me a wish today
And if it could only be one
I know exactly what I'd wish for
To be together with my son!

I don't know anything that would make me happier
I would feel joyful, it's true
Just knowing ours lives would be
Eternal Praising the Lord is what we'd do!

To walk all through Heaven
And see my family that's there
Knowing that they have been waiting for me
To show me the beauty, everywhere!

They would tell me about their life there
And that my son's had a eye out for me
So excited that I was coming
He knew we'd be there for Eternity!

My son was my only one
I had love enough for more
Sometimes I imagine him coming home
Just walking through that door!

So special he was to me
I'll never forget that smile
And if I could tell him something
I'd tell him I'll be home in a little while!

Diamonds in the Rough

Pain We've Never Felt

Parents should never have to bury their child
It's just a feeling like you've never felt
It puts you in shock for a good while
You heart is torn to pieces, no doubt!

I have my son's ashes that I haven't spread yet
I went to the beach but, couldn't
Just thinking it's throwing my baby away
To get rid of him, I shouldn't!

So for now they sit up on my shelf
And my husbands too
Maybe someday I will be ready
Maybe it's what I should do!

This has been the most trying time
That I've ever been through
I've never felt pain this strong
I felt this was coming, I knew!

A mother has a way of knowing
When things are just not right
Especially with her children
Even in the middle of the night!

I felt one day my son would leave
It had been on his mind for years
When I heard him talk about it
It just put me in tears!

Diamonds in the Rough

I know where he is now
And I wouldn't have it any other way
Because I know he's finally at peace
And I'll see him again someday!

Diamonds in the Rough

God's Promise To Us

I want to help people with my poems
I want to help them cope
On the days that are the hardest
I want to offer them some hope!

The hope I have is in the Lord
He's promised to get me through
He says He'll walk through the fire with me
And I know His promises are true!

I'm going to put together a book about grief
Someday I'll get it done
I hope it won't take too long
It will be a tribute to my son!

I know my words will bring some comfort
Like they always do for me
Because we're all grieving the same
That's very easy to see!

Somedays will bring much sadness to us
When we are thinking about our child
The nights sometimes get lonely
We'll be grieving for awhile!

I learned of Gods assurance
That I'll someday see my son
What a day I look forward to
When my work on this Earth is done!

Diamonds in the Rough

By Your Side, He'll Stay

Months ago my body was heavy
It felt like it was weighed down with stones
No one really to talk to
I was feeling so all alone!

Grieving is a a difficult process
Never knowing when the waves will come
They can be quite powerful
And leave us feeling numb!

I know feeling numb protects us
But soon all of it ends
We know what lies ahead
Through tragedy we have been!

I can't imagine what I would do
If God wasn't by my side
He let's me know that He's right here
In me He does abide!

I'm so thankful that I have these groups
That get me through difficult days
They're kind and understanding
For them I go to God and pray!

I ask Him to get them through
Each and everyday
Through the pain and heartache
And if by their side He'll stay!

Diamonds in the Rough

Reminiscing

My little boy would pick me flowers in the spring
And throw leaves at me in the fall
We had some fun during this season
It's my favorite one of all!

I'm sitting here remeneizing
About my son when he was young
He was quite a character
At the top of his lungs, he sung!

If I could just have those years back
Instead of being in this pain
I would have held his hand a little longer
And played together in the rain!

I didn't know that he'd leave so young
To make it to Heaven before me
The Lord saw his wounded heart
Long before I could ever see!

Heaven will give us another chance
To spend time together once more
He'll tell me about his time there
And how he's happier than ever before!

Although my heart is still heavy
It cheers me up to know
That my son has a Glorified body
And God is loving him so!

Diamonds in the Rough

Each Day Brings Me Closer

I'm staring at your picture on my dresser
And realize it's the best one I have of you
Also there's a cap hanging on the door
Much grieving is what I do!

I look at your face and there's no smile
You were trying to celebrate your birthday
Many of your pictures all looked the same
That helped me understand why you couldn't stay!

It doesn't feel good to see your child unhappy
But sometimes it just turns out that way
God says there'll be trials and tribulations
Some suffer here everyday!

I'm just so sad my son had to leave
Although I understood his mind
A troubled boy early in his life
Just peace I wanted him to find!

I'll never blame him for leaving
Because he's in an amazing place
And he tried the best he could
Now God's given him mercy and grace!

I know it will seem like a long time
Before his face, I'll see
But each day draws me closer
To Heaven where I'll one day be!

Diamonds in the Rough

My Son's Glorious Home

I have bled all my life
Because my heart's been torn
Years of trials and tribulations
I'm tired now, I'm worn!

Losing my son was the worst so far
Such a tremendous amount of pain
Going to the core of my soul
Tears coming down like rain!

Why does it have to hurt so bad
And break our hearts in two?
We all are in this together
And I truly empathize with you!

I know the day will come
When maybe we'll start to mend
But I know that will take awhile
Because down a hard road we've been!

I realize if my son came back
He wouldn't want to stay
He'd never want to leave his Heavenly home
Where he's been since that Glorious day!

I know my pain will be for a bit longer
And I trust God to get me through
This tragedy caught me by surprise
But the Lord already knew!

Diamonds in the Rough

A Life Of Splendor

Another Saturday has come and gone
And I'm not too happy about this day
Because it brings back the horrific memory
Of that Saturday you passed away!

A little time has gone by now
And a spark of light I'm beginning to see
Thinking about where my son is
Knowing he's as happy as can be!

I just try to imagine the peace he has
Since he entered Heaven that day
I am so thankful to the Lord for that
My son has joy that will never fade away!

So much love he is feeling now
Love like he's never felt before
God's wrapping His arms around him
And giving him more, so much more!

If I could have witnessed my sons arrival
I would've been as thrilled as could be
Knowing he's living a life of splendor
A wonderful sight to see!

My sons new life he's enjoying
And someday I will be too
I felt he would get to Heaven before me
In my heart I just knew!

Diamonds in the Rough

I'm Thinking Back

I'm thinking back years ago
When my son was just a boy
I'd put him to bed, kiss his face
And tell him a bible story!

I'll never forget his childhood
Some happy times we had
He was surely a mama's boy
But had good times with his dad!

I taught him what I thought he should know
I did the best that I could
I helped him with his problems
Like any mother would!

But sometimes my help wasn't enough
And that made me really sad
There were many days that were trying
Because of the mental illness that he had!

I saw as he got older, it got worse
A very troubled mind
I felt so helpless all of the time
Peace I just wanted him to find!

He's found his peace that I prayed for
God finally set him free
Someday I will be there too
What a Glorious day that will be!

Diamonds in the Rough

God Gives Me His Strength

This doesn't seem real to me
How can you just be gone?
The rest of my life without you
Sometimes it's hard to carry on!

But I know I will survive this
Although it's the worst I've ever felt
I know the Lord will give me His strength
And this I have no doubt!

Now my son is gone from this world
I'm trying to accept it somehow
It's so hard to get through this
My heart is broken right now!

A little while has gone by
But it feels like yesterday
That I got the shattering news
I was in shock, had nothing to say!

If there ever was a time I needed God the most
It's right now as the months go by
But knowing that He'll pull me through
And He sees the tears that I cry!

I know this pain I have in my soul
May soften up someday
The Lord continues to give me His strength
It's truly the only way!

Diamonds in the Rough

His Precious Face I'll See

I'm sitting here missing my boy
I just miss him oh, so much
I want to feel him here with me
And his body I want to touch!

I cry out to God and tell Him how much it hurts
And I know He sees my tears
He knows how much I've suffered
This could last many years!

I just can't believe my child is gone
How long before I can hold him tight
I'm trying not to cry so much
I'm putting up a pretty good fight!

But maybe I should just let it out
Whether anyone sees me or not
It's so hard holding these tears back
I just cry an awful lot!

Most people don't know the heartache
That we parents suffer through
And if it happened to them
They probably wouldn't know what to do!

I know my son isn't suffering now
And maybe he's even keeping an eye on me
Making sure I'm doing alright
Until his precious face I see!

Diamonds in the Rough

I Hope My Love Was Enough

The days and nights are moving so fast
 I feel I'm being pushed away from you
I hope the love I gave was enough
Missing you is all I can do!

As time moves on, I'll miss you more
Sometimes it just doesn't seem real
That on this Earth I won't see you again
And so sad is how I feel!

On the loneliest nights I'm thinking about you
And how it all turned out to be
But then I think, I'm in Gods hands
And He's really taking care of me!

He sees me sitting here in my chair
I just look out of the window and think
Wondering how long this pain will last
If any lower, can I sink?

The Lord hears my desperate plea
He sees the tears in my eyes
And He knows that I'm thinking back
To the day I told you goodbye!

God is leading me through this grief
And He's doing it His way
I know I can let go and trust Him
To get me through each day!

Diamonds in the Rough

Peace And Joy We'll Find

If I hadn't been through pain and heartache
From my past and up until now
I couldn't write poems about grief and suffering
I really wouldn't know how!

God has given me a special gift
By using my pain and tears
To write these poems that help some
I write about heartache and fear!

I am joyful in knowing that my writings help you all
You say, they bring much comfort to you
I appreciate this gift God's given
And I'll continue to write these poems that are true!

I don't want my pain to be wasted
When I know I can help people out
There are all you mothers that are hurting
And I know what grief and suffering are about!

Some of you are wondering why God has allowed
A tragedy that you're going through
A loss of a daughter or son
Grieving for them is all you can do!

I really don't know the answer to that
I wish I could ease your mind
But I know someday that answer will come
And peace and joy we'll find!

Diamonds in the Rough

If I Could Reach To Heaven

If I could reach to Heaven
And bring you back again
Just to stay for awhile
I think my heart would start to mend!

I miss you so very much
My heart doesn't know what to do
The tears keep flowing from my eyes
Every time I think of you!

I know the reason that you left
And I couldn't make you stay
I know your mind was troubled
On that day that you passed away!

I just wish you had come to me
And told me what you were going through
I would've tried to understand
And gotten you some help too!

Well, it's all over now
And you're finally set free
I know your home in Heaven
Is the place I want to be!

Diamonds in the Rough

Experiencing Heaven

My son believed in God like I taught him
And I know he often said a prayer
To get him through his struggles
Pain and suffering he had to bear!

I know it was more than he could handle
And I prayed for him everyday
That the Lord would take care of him
I didn't know any other way!

I've never been bitter for what has happened
Although my heart's been broken into
God in His wisdom, years ago
Knew what my son would do!

For some reason he was born with this illness
A disease that he fought for years
I really didn't know how to help him
I saw him fight the pain and tears!

This life can be unfair sometimes
Problems for each and everyone
I just didn't have the answers then
To help my troubled son!

I know where he is and I'm happy
That he doesn't have to suffer anymore
He's now experiencing the gift of Heaven
And waiting to see what God has in store!

Diamonds in the Rough

God's In Control

When pain and loneliness is all I know
The Lord comes and takes it from me
He sees me in my sufferings
And peaceful He wants me to be!

This journey I'm on isn't easy
Most people have no idea
The rough terrain, the mountains I climb
I'm just surprised that I'm still here!

But I won't give up that easy
Because I've been down hard roads before
Although sometimes I feel so weary and worn
And think I can't take anymore!

God tells me that I will come threw this
Although He's seen many tears I cry
He knows how broken my heart is
Because I had to tell my son, goodbye!

The answer to this tragedy, I try to find
But God tells me that only He knows
He says that I'll know the answer someday
And He knows how I love my son so!

I won't try to figure out things on my own
Because my God is in control
And I know He loves me, oh so much
I can feel it down in my soul!

Diamonds in the Rough

I Decided

I decided I needed to cry today
Let the flood of tears run out
Just pulling thoughts out of my mind
Until my heart starts to melt!

I decided that maybe I didn't know my son
The way I really wanted to
Although I saw the pain and tears
The suffering he was going through!

I decided that maybe it wasn't my fault
That my son chose to leave that way
I only wish that I could have helped him
It just eats at me everyday!

I decided I want to help the ones suffering
And brighten up their light that's gone dim
Tell about the love God has
And how He really adores them!

I decided I won't be angry at God
For taking my son, so young
He knows things I'll never know
Since before the world began!

I decided I'll stay here until I'm called home
When at last I'll be set free
No pain or suffering, no more tears
With my family is where I want to be!

Diamonds in the Rough

Real Peace I Will Find

My mother and father, husband and son
Are strolling through Heaven together
It just thrills my soul to know one day
That I'll be there with them forever!

This life here is hard sometimes
And bad things happen to us
When I lost my son a year ago
In the Lord I put my trust!

It wasn't easy to do that
Because I had questions in my mind
Although these questions I never asked Him
Peace I just wanted to find!

God knew all about what happened
And someday He'll reveal it to me
Why He allowed such a tragedy
Why it was His will to set him free!

I feel calm and peaceful that my son is with the Lord
But it's just hard to wait until my time comes
As long as I'm here, the tears will remain
And my heart will sometimes feel numb!

I'll never blame God for what happened
Because His ways are not mine
I know one day with my son I will be
And there, real peace I will find!

Diamonds in the Rough

God Has Kept Me Strong

Come and take me Lord when you are ready
Then I can be with my son
I know he will know I'm coming
And through those pearly gates he'll run!

I'll hold him, oh so tight
And I will kiss his face
And tell him how much I missed him
Since he's been in this wonderful place!

I'm not saying I'm ready to leave this world
Because they're things that need to be done
The Lord has called me to serve Him
Before I reunite with my son!

This life is very short down here
So I need to tell people of Gods love
And the strength that He gives us when we're grieving
For our loved ones up above!

It's so hard to lose a part of ourselves
That we've had for many years
A precious son or daughter
We lose count of the many tears!

I've been here on Earth for many years
I'm grateful God has let me live this long
Although I've been through trials and tribulations
He had kept me strong!

Diamonds in the Rough

Seeing Him Face To Face

A nice service we had for my brother today
I just can't believe he went so quick
The good Lord was ready for him
He knew he was weary and sick!

Tears ran down my face as I cried
Knowing in this life I wouldn't see him again
Feeling the part he played in my life
A good brother to me, he'd been!

As I looked around I saw others
Trying to hide their tears
A flood of grief seeping out
My brother they held so dear!

A nice poem of mine was written
Only a few days ago
It told of the excitement of Heaven
My brother now surely knows!

Even though we will all miss him
We must see him in a Heavenly place
Praising his Heavenly Father
And finally meeting Him face to face!

Diamonds in the Rough

God Whispered His Name

We all gather today to say goodbye
To a man that was after Gods own heart
A true Christian and a gentle soul
Our hearts are saddened to be apart!

Goodbyes are never easy
Even though we know they're with the Lord
Years and years of loving them
This was a man we all adored!

He was such a kind and compassionate person
A sweet brother to me indeed
There were times he helped me out
When I was down and had a need!

He tried to do more than his share
And he spread himself so thin
Always thinking about others
There to help them he had been!

My brother was truly one in a million
A real special kind of guy
The night the Lord took him home
I never ask the question of why!

I knew in my heart it was his time
The Lord knew he was ready to go
So He leaned over and whispered his name
We love and will miss him so!

Diamonds in the Rough

His Shining Light

Another summer has come and gone
And my mind is still on you
It seems like its been a long year
But the Lord is getting me through!

I'm going into the second year
Some say it's worse than before
I really hope this isn't true
Because I don't know if I can take anymore!

I'm sitting in the bedroom that use to be yours
And I've turned it into mine
I just wanted to feel close to you
Some peace I just want to find!

I'm not ready to spread your ashes
At the beach and off the pier
I just want to keep you close to me
I really want to feel you here!

Your death is the worst I've ever felt
And I've really suffered before
Although I've had many losses
This one cuts me to the core!

I have to follow the path this grief leads me
And I can't see the end in sight
When this happens I turn to God
And He leads me with his shining light!

Diamonds in the Rough

A Place I Long To Go

Sometimes God gives me a glimpse of Heaven
It only last for a minute or two
A peace in my heart that I've never known
It makes me feel closer to you!

What a privilege to experience Heaven
It's where my loved ones go
Most important, Jesus is there
Whom, I do love so!

Son, I have no doubt God took you home
To a place He's prepared for you
What a wonderful Paradise
One day it will be mine too!

I can't imagine a place of peace
With no more pain and tears
Just forever praising the Lord
And feeling Him so near!

I know you're there with God now
You're praising the King Of Kings
Never to come back to this place
Just there hearing the Angels sing!

I just can't wait to join you
A place that I've Longed to go
There with Jesus loving me
And this I surely know!

Diamonds in the Rough

One day my heart will mend
When I step through those pearly gates
The Lord in His goodness has promised this
And He is never a day late!

Diamonds in the Rough

You're In Paradise

The brilliant sun comes up each morning
Followed by a beautiful sunset that appears
I think of the beauty of our Earth
And at times I feel you near!

I think it's because you're experiencing much beauty too
I would love to see the sights there
God created it just so perfect
And His artwork is everywhere!

I feel happy that you're with your Heavenly Father
Bringing you home is what He chose to do
Away from a life of pain
Love and peace God's given to you!

I wondered how long you would go on like that
And I didn't know how you'd get through
Much pain in your heart and mind
You never knew what to do!

I feel better that You're now in peace
You've searched for it for years
My heart was broken from watching you
Go through the pain and tears!

I loved you more than life, my son
Would I call you back to stay?
I wouldn't because you're in paradise
And I'll see you again one day!

Diamonds in the Rough

Peace Of Mind

Sad feelings come and they go
And this is every day
It's never been this bad before
I think they're here to stay!

I've never grieved this long before
Grieving for my husband, I got through
But this is so much different
I'm just sad because I'm grieving for you!

I know my son wouldn't want me to hurt
But it's so hard to push the pain away
When I awake in the morning, there it is
Just feeling like it's going to stay!

I feel tired now and I feel worn
I'm lucky if I remember my name
Since this tragedy, alot has changed
And I'll never be the same!

There's no going back to the old me
The person I was has faded away
I might smile and I might laugh
But this new me is here to stay!

I'll continue on this journey
And pray that I see the signs
It won't be easy, but I must try
To give me peace of mind!

Diamonds in the Rough

God Knew What Was Best For You

I have a picture of you, in my mind
And I can see that smile on your face
I have no doubt that you're at peace
I also vision that Glorious place!

I'm so relieved that you're in Heaven
And your dad's happy to see you too
The best part is that you met the Lord
And He has so much love for you!

My mind can never comprehend
Such an Eternal home for me
Where God's love and peace are there
When I get there I will see!

I know son you have so much joy
Like you have never had before
God has promised you an Eternal future
And He had so much in store!

I realize that I need to let you go
But it's such a hard thing to do
I've cried so many tears
And I cry them just for you!

I know you left this world too soon
But God knew what was best for you
He wanted to rid you of your pain and tears
And give you a body brand new!

Diamonds in the Rough

I Wonder

I wonder if my son can hear me laugh
If he can see my every tear
Does he know that I'm longing for him
That I want to feel him near?

I wonder if he knows my heart is broken?
Since that tragic day
Does he know that I've ask the Lord
To just wash this pain away?

I wonder if he knows how I'm feeling?
That sometimes there's guilt on my mind
I wish that I could've helped him more
So joy and happiness he could find!

I wonder if he's listening to Angels playing their harps?
If he's joining in with them to sing?
I know he feels Heaven is the most wonderful place
Because of the peace and love God brings!

I wonder if his loved ones were waiting at the gate for him?
Did he recognize everyone?
Were there children in the meadow
Just laughing and having fun?

I wonder when he first laid eyes on Jesus
Did it just take his breath away?
Was he just mesmerized by His beauty
And couldn't find one word to say?

Diamonds in the Rough

I think my son experiences all these things
And I know he's there waiting for me
He's asking the Lord to bring me home someday
So, in Heaven we'll forever be!

Diamonds in the Rough

My Funny Boy

My son, Travis was quite a prankster
Always playing jokes on me
And every time I'd fall for it
So tickled he would be!

He always wanted to be a cop
Since he was a little guy
Those blue and red lights just fascinated him
Joining the force he wanted to try!

So he attended school for over a year
And then just dropped out one day
He said his depression wouldn't let him finish
I thought there had to be a different way!

Then he managed to join the fire department
And they made him an EMT
He'd come by and blow that horn
And he'd just smile at me!

He installed red and blue lights in his car
And just stayed outside and watched them
He said he was scared to drive with them on
Because he knew they would ticket him!

Well, I had gone out that evening
And when I came home it was night
I pulled in my driveway and looked
In my mirror and saw these lights!

Diamonds in the Rough

I didn't have my license with me
And a ticket I didn't want to pay
I shouldn't have left without it
I wished I hadn't gone out that day!

So I was feeling very anxious
The cop was just sitting there
I didn't know why he was taking so long
Then I said a prayer!

I looked in my mirror and saw him get out
And he was walking in a funny way
He came to my window and I stuck my head out
He said, I got you mom, April Fools Day!

There were times when he was happy
He would write funny poems like me
Now I bet he's having fun in Heaven
One day I will see!

Diamonds in the Rough

You're Finally Happy Where You Are

You weren't much on conversation
But I just wish I had talked to you more
I wanted to dig deep into your heart
Because I knew you were fighting a war!

Day in and day out
I just felt it was unfair to you
I sensed what was going on in your mind
And I longed to get you help too!

If you would have just given me a chance
If you could've just talked to me
I was more than willing to help you
Because healthy I wanted you to be!

I could feel the depression you were suffering from
Because I've been down that road before
It's the hardest thing to deal with
You feel like you can't take anymore!

I know there was medicine out there
Because I found some that finally worked for me
How great it was to get some relief
The Lord finally set me free!

Well, I know you're happy where you are
And this pain, God's getting me through
He's promised to take me there some day
I just love and miss you too!

Diamonds in the Rough

He's In My Heart

I read his autopsy report tonight
And I did better than I thought
It just said what I knew it would
Now I have pain seeping out of my heart!

Some friends told me not to read it
But I didn't listen to them
I just felt in my soul
That I needed closure with him!

I do feel a little better
Just knowing the facts were true
It's just something I needed to know about
Just something I needed to do!

Well, that's done and over with
And I won't have to wonder anymore
My son is with the Lord now
So much happier than before!

This extremely hard road that I'm going down
Doesn't seem to have an end
But I'm not going to stop for anything
In this tragedy, I'm going to win!

I pray that my pain slows down over time
But I don't know if that will be true
All I know that he's in this heart to stay
And I just love and miss him too!

Diamonds in the Rough

My Gift God's Given Me

If I had a dollar for each tear
I've cried I would be a millionaire
But then money can't make you happy
Or take away this pain I bear!

No one can take it away but the Lord himself
I've been counting on Him for years
Each tragedy that I've been through
He's there to wipe away each tear!

God doesn't want us to suffer
But trials and tribulations will come
He sees my heart so broken
And the pain has made me numb!

This life is harsh and suffering is rough
And I can't do it on my own
I cry out to God in a desperate plea
When I'm in pain and all alone!

He knows the depth of my heartache
And He knows that He's made me strong
He lets me know that I'll make it through
Even though this suffering seems so wrong!

God, in my pain and heartache
Has given me a gift
I feel It is my desire to help others
I want to help them heal!

Diamonds in the Rough

I'll See You In A Different Light

Your beautiful urn made of blue and white marble
Was heavy and hard to get down
I've never opened it in a year and a few months
Your ashes just make me feel you're around!

I cried ofcourse like I always do
Just to see it sitting on my shelf
I'm just sitting here in my room
Just weeping and by myself!

My son left a child just like him
He has brought me so much joy
He's all I have left of him
And he is quite a special boy!

We don't talk about his dad
Because he knows what happened that day
He's always kept his feelings to himself
And at times doesn't have much to say!

I feel that oneday He'll come around
And want to know more about his dad
He keeps his memories in his heart
Of some good times they had!

I'm ready to put this urn back on the shelf
I've cried enough for one night
And maybe get it down in awhile
And see my son in a different light!

Diamonds in the Rough

Only The Lord Knows

I open my mouth to cry sometimes
And no sound inside comes out
I just have days when it's too much
And I want to scream and shout!

This grief is just so lonely
I just want to talk about my son
No one wants to talk about him
I guess they think my grieving should be done!

Well, I have good news for them
I'll never talk about my son again
They can't understand anyway
They don't know the road I've been!

Yes, it's been a hard road to travel
People don't have any idea
The suffering and heartache that comes
I just want my child right here!

I need for people to be patient with me
Because I'm still fighting these storms
After awhile it calms down
Then another big wave takes form!

I don't mean to feel sad and unhappy
My broken heart just comes and goes
There's only one person that can hear my plea
Yes, only the good Lord knows!

Diamonds in the Rough

Our Faith

I taught you to have faith in God
When you were old enough to understand
I told you how much He loved you
And for your life He had a plan!

A plan that He could see for you
He had it all worked out
So I set and read with you
So you'd understand what it was all about!

We read the bible every night
There was so much he wanted to know
I explained to him the best I could

And I told him how God loved him so!
He reached his teens and asked why God didn't help him
Because he was feeling a troubled mind
He realized that he wasn't living like others
That he was then far behind!

He remembered the faith I had taught him
And he knew that it was real
But he questioned me again about God's plan
Joy and happiness he didn't feel!

I stuck with him until the end
And I struggled about what to do
It was totally out of my hands
In God's wisdom, He knew!

Diamonds in the Rough

My faith during my grief has never faltered
God's plan I understand
He knew that my boy was ready
Now He has him in His hands!

Diamonds in the Rough

We'll Forever Stay

You gracefully folded you little hands
And said a mealtime prayer
You weren't ashamed or embarrassed
When we went to eat, anywhere!

I always taught you to thank the Lord
For the food that we had
I told you that some people don't have any
And that made you very sad!

You were really a good boy
And I miss the times with you
But God decided to let you go
And be reunited with your dad, too!

Of course I'm sad because you're gone
And I'm sure it will last a long while
I try to think about the happy times
When you were just a child!

The Lord knew you needed to go
To His Heaven where you'd be free
I'm really feel joyful knowing you're at peace
But it surely got the best of me!

You live on my son in Paradise
And I will join you someday
We'll have some catching up to do
And we'll have Eternity there to stay!

Diamonds in the Rough

I'll Cherish The Memories

A little part of me is in Heaven
Because you are there
Just so happy and peaceful
And no burdens for you to bear!

I just wish I could get a glimpse of where you are
I know you haven't been there too long
Just surrounded by the Angels
And listening to such beautiful songs!

I'm so excited that I'll be there someday
But I don't know when that will be
I know the Lord has work in store
And then He'll set me free!

I'll be mesmerized in that holy place
A place that I've longed to go
So many beautiful sights to see
And I'll see you there, I know!

You were a special son to me
And now I carry you in my heart
I'll always cherish the times we had
And the joy to me, you brought!

Diamonds in the Rough

I'm Trying To Imagine

I'm trying to imagine when your soul left your body
That you must have felt freedom at last
No pain, or suffering, no more tears
Everything healed from your past!

What an awesome adventure it was
When the Angels carried you up on high
Seeing the Lord that you've longed to meet
And telling this world goodbye!

I know Heaven had been on your mind alot
You were so ready for God to take you
You never told that to me
But in my heart, I already knew!

I knew it was your time to go to your Heavenly home
To meet your Creator there
Oh, the sights you must have seen
Angles flying everywhere!

To just be there with family
And just feeling so mesmerized
Just to see your Savior face to face
Seeing the love in His eyes!

I look so forward to feeling that love there
And I can't wait until I see you
The Lord has you in His arms
I really love and miss you too!
Donna Carpenter August 12th 2020 For My Brother, Wayne

Diamonds in the Rough

I'll See You Soon

Please, meet me at those pearly gates
And bring our son with you
I know that you've been waiting for me
And I want to see Jesus too!

You don't know how long I've waited
And you don't know how much I've cried
When you left it just broke my heart
It really tore me up inside!

It's been awhile since you've been gone
But our son just gained his wings
I know y'all are there, enjoying your new home
And feeling the love God brings!

Sometimes I have dreams of you
But I wake up and know it isn't real
I just wanted it to last forever
But saddened is how I feel!

Our son is now living in perfect peace
We couldn't ask for anything more
God is really taking care of him
More than He ever has before!

I'll try to move on some, and not be sad
Because my life down here will end
And it won't be too long until I'm with you
And we'll be happier than we've ever been!

Diamonds in the Rough

A Window To Heaven

If there was a window to Heaven
And we could see the Angels there
With their wings spread out
And our children in their care!

What an awesome moment that would be
To see the peacefulness on our child's face
To just know they're not in pain
Because God's brought them to an Eternal place!

I just can't comprehend the sight it will be
And a love like we've never known
To just have one big family
And to never be alone!

The Lord is so good to me
He's just been with me the whole way
He knows how much I miss my son
And He promises me to see him again one day!

I know my son just longed for Heaven
Although he didn't say much about it to me
I could tell it in his actions
Just without suffering he wanted to be!

I can't really blame him for leaving
I know what he had on his mind
He asked the Lord to take him home
And leave this world behind!

Diamonds in the Rough

In Heaven, Up On High

I always knew that you'd leave this way
To relieve the suffering in your mind
Just pain and heartache for so many years
Happiness you just couldn't find!

I just think about your feelings
And the pain you had to bear
I knew there was nothing that I could do
So I always kept you in my prayers!

I know the Lord knew the answer
He knew you inside and out
He was sad as He watched you struggle
Grieving is how He felt!

I know where you are and you're peaceful
And sometimes that helps my pain
But other times my tears just flood
They come down like the fallen rain!!

I've never felt heartache like this before
Even though I've suffered for years
And I've never cried this much
I just want to feel you near!

I thank God that He blessed me with you
You were the apple of my eye
I can't wait to see you again
You're in Heaven up on high!

Diamonds in the Rough

I'll Be There In A While

You've been gone for over a year
And you've really started to live
Just there sitting at Jesus's side
And feeling the peace He gives!

What a day it will be in Heaven
Oh, what joy I will feel
To see you and your dad together
And to know that you've been healed!

Healed from your Earthly problems
No more pain to bear
No heartache or suffering, no more tears
Just spending Eternity there!

God has been a blessing to me
He has been right here all along
He sees my pain and tears
And He gives help to make me strong!

I wish I could be close to you like the Angels are
And see the excitement in your eyes
For one day we will be together
And I'll never have to tell you goodbye!

So really enjoy the depth of God's love
And just keep an eye out for me
Because I'll be there in a little while
And you will have Eternity with me!

Diamonds in the Rough

What A Reunion

You ask me how I'm doing
I say to you, not bad
I don't want you to see my pain
That makes me really sad!

I think about my son alot
He's always on my mind
Thinking about what a good person he was
Handsome, sweet, and kind!

I would just love to see him
And the peace that God has given
And see a big smile on his face
In Heaven and really living!

There will always be a special place in my heart
And the memories, I have them too
Memories of our time together
Oh, how I treasured you!

The time is going by fast since you've been gone
But it's not taking away this grief
I'm just learning to live with it
And hoping one day I'll get relief!

You were such a special gift to me
The Lord gave me a beautiful boy
I waited for you for so long
And I was so filled with joy!

Diamonds in the Rough

I'll see you again, I'm sure of
And what a reunion that will be
I'll finally meet my Savior
Who willingly died for me!

Diamonds in the Rough

You're Dear to God's Heart

I wish that I could've made you better
So you could stay a little longer
I know that the Lord could've helped you
To make your mind a little stronger!

I know the Lord knew your pain
He saw the sadness in your eyes
He knew you had suffered for years and years
And He knew we'd have to tell you goodbye!

I have so many memories of you
Down through the years
At times you seemed so happy
And other times you were in tears!

There has to be a good reason
That God wanted you here
You are His son and He knows you well
And in His heart, He holds you dear!

I know you're so happy where you are
And you're longing for me to come
I feel so happy and thrilled sometimes
But other times I feel numb!

Always remember how much I love you
And we'll see each other again someday
I loved the person that you were
You had such compassionate ways!

Diamonds in the Rough

God Is Never Late

God knew your mind wasn't well
So He took you home with Him
He saw you suffering even more
He saw the light in your soul go dim!

As much as I miss you, I am thankful
That the Lord allowed you to go
Your pain you always hid well
Most people didn't even know!

Alot of people know about this disease
And others don't have a clue
I feel so bad that you inherited from me
This illness started when you were two!

The main two things I instilled in you
Were to love God with all your heart
And to know the depth of my love
Even though we have to be apart!

I just seem to be missing you more
And thinking about your dad, too
But then I just picture you in that Holy City
Where there are clouds, and the sky is so blue!

You're going to know without doubt, when I arrive
Because I'm running through the pearly gates
And you'll definitely know that it's my time
Because God is never late!

Diamonds in the Rough

God's Love Is The Best

I loved my boy with all my heart
From the moment he opened his eyes
I didn't know his life would be cut short
And I wouldn't get to tell him goodbye!

Maybe I should move along with it
Although sad, I'll always be
My son is surely in a better place
Because the Lord has set him free!

His mind isn't suffering anymore
And he now has a reason to live
There's nowhere better that he could be
Just feeling the love God gives!

There are questions I need to ask the Lord
Things that I need to understand
Like why He allowed my boy to leave so young
Why was in in His plan!

I sorta already know the answer
It really wasn't His idea
But He saw my son just suffering
So He decided to not leave him here!

God already knew the outcome
And my son made peace with Him one night
My son knew that he might end his life
And he wanted to make things right!

Diamonds in the Rough

I think about him night and day
And I know that will always be
Even though he's not here right now
When I get to Heaven, I'll see!

I'll know then why God took him home
It's because his mind needed some rest
And what better place to be
Then with God, who's love is the best!

Diamonds in the Rough

He's in Heaven

Forever I prayed for my babies before they were born
I ask God to keep them in His care
He blessed me with a daughter and son
Although an illness he had to bear!

My son started out just being peculiar
And then it got worse when he was three
He had to be on medication
A happy child I wanted him to be!

Most of the time he didn't smile
I knew something was really wrong
Although he loved to sing
Walking around singing bible songs!

I asked the Lord why he had to suffer
I just didn't understand His plan
I knew He allowed it for a reason
And I know He had him in His hands!

As he got older, things got worse
He broke windows when his dad passed away
I didn't know how to help him
I dealt with his problems everyday!

The depression just grew worse as he aged
Getting angry and punching walls
Shouting that he didn't want to live
He'd just go to his room and bawl!

Diamonds in the Rough

Seeing him like this just broke my heart
I just wanted to help him get through
I knew it wasn't going to get better
So I didn't know what to do!

I suspected anytime, he'd take his life
I prayed it wouldn't be in his room
So much suffering he went through
He just felt his life was doomed!

Now as I look back, I did everything
To make his life be better
But I knew it wasn't enough
Now he's in Heaven with his dad, forever!

Diamonds in the Rough

His Dream

My little boy loved police cars
And all kind of fire trucks
He told me he'd someday drive one
For me to wish him luck!

I told him he could do what he put his mind to
And don't forget that the Lord has plans
He longs for you to fulfill them
And He holds you in His hands!

The years went by and he finished school
And was ready to start his dream
He was excepted with no problems
Quite an eager fireman it seemed!

He was good at what he did
He made this mama so proud
Sometimes he'd ride by in his truck
And toot the horn so loud!

Soon after he started, there were problems
But he never let them be known
Guys at the station thought he was quite normal
But on the inside he felt alone!

I knew his illness had never left
The meds calmed it down for awhile
I'd see him outside late at night
I'd bet he'd walked a mile!

Diamonds in the Rough

He was never in a position to support himself
Because the job he loved was volunteer
He couldn't keep a regular job
So he just stayed with me right here!

He gave the fire department seven years
Then they had to let him go
He wasn't showing up for drills or meetings
His depression they didn't know!

The year before he took his life
I started seeing him go downhill
I suggested he see a doctor
But living wasn't his will!

I know that he's been set so free
And he knows that Heaven is real
I would give anything to see him
So joyful I would feel!

Diamonds in the Rough

He's Resting In Jesus

My little boy asked me where Heaven was
I told him it was way up top on the sky
He asked why we couldn't see it there
And will we go there when we die?

I told him we'd get a Glorious body
One that would never grow old
No pain or sickness or heartache
Just a wonderful body to hold!

Through the years he asked lots of questions
About Jesus and Heaven and such
He knew someday he'd go there
And be healed by the Masters touch!

He knew he had a problem
One that most people couldn't see
He tried to cover it up the best he could
Just a normal boy he wanted to be!

More years went by and he grew up
And still his mind wasn't well
As he remembered everything I'd taught him about God
Down to his knees, he just fell!

He asked God to forgive him
Because he didn't want to live anymore
Heaven just seemed like an awesome place
So what was he fighting for?

Diamonds in the Rough

I know these thoughts he was feeling that night
And I know with God, he'd made peace
I just wish I could've see him in Heaven
When the Lord made his pain be released!

Every time I start thinking sad thoughts
I bring this image into my mind
The minute I see him again
So much peace and joy I'll find!

Diamonds in the Rough

Their Hearts Are Saddened

He had too much to drink that night
As he ran the stop sign
She didn't see him coming
As he crossed the yellow line!

She was just a kid, going on seventeen
Her life had only begun
What a horrible tragedy it was
Because now her life is done!

She had plans for a bright future
She loved working with kids
A dream to become a doctor
But that's shattered because of what he did!

Now, what are her parents to do
She was their only girl
They tried for more but couldn't
Bad things happen in this world!

Who knows if they'll ever find this man
He just hit her hard and ran
He shouldn't have taken that drink
I just don't understand!

So now her parents are saddened
How they miss her so much every day
Being so close to the Lord
They just bow their heads and pray!

Diamonds in the Rough

In the Presence Of God

I cried a little while today
I couldn't get him off my mind
I knew when my son reached Heaven
Love and happiness he'd find!

It's good for him because he's been set free
But I am left down here
Here to just cry my eyes out
I just want to feel him near!

I really don't want to complain too much
Because my boy is in a wonderful place
There with Jesus and his dad
And a smile upon his face!

I don't want to seem ungrateful
But I feel he left too soon
Although deep down I already knew
That his mind was an open wound!

Not enough strength to carry on
Or maybe he didn't want to stay
I'd taught him all about the Lord
And how He'd take him home one day!

So my son chose Heaven over this world
Maybe he made the right choice
To be in the presence of God
And to hear the Angles voice!

Diamonds in the Rough

This Illness

My son fought his mental illness
A normal boy, he'd never been
He was different when he was with his friends
He tried his best to pretend!

People in the last stage of depression are taking their lives
And other people are losing their fight
Both really want to stay in this world
And they push hard with all their might!

Some think mental illness is different
It's one people don't talk about
It makes them feel ashamed
No respect have they ever felt!

My son tried to have a normal life
But in my heart I already knew
That he would never find that peace he wanted
And I felt there was nothing that I could do!

If I could've had just a little more time
If I could've made him see
That there was help out there for him
That maybe would've set him free!

Although I wish I'd had pushed him harder
A better life he could've had
But now when I think about him in Heaven
Then I'm happy, not always sad!

Diamonds in the Rough

I'll Embrace Them

Someday the Lord will call me home
And I'll see him face to face
What a wonderful day that will be
And my family I will finally embrace!

I miss my husband and son so much
I wish we didn't have to be apart
Sometimes this grief is so hard
I feel I'm missing a piece of my heart!

I didn't know I'd lose them so soon
With our life I had alot of plans
Somedays when I'm feeling so down
Why they left, I don't understand!

But, on other days I know the answer
It's easy to plainly see
That they were ready to leave this world
Heaven is where they Longed to be!

I know that they didn't suffer
On the days they passed away
The Lord softly called them home
So with Him they could forever stay!

I'm so looking forward to Heaven
Where God will wipe my tears away
No more pain or suffering
Oh what a wonderful day!

Diamonds in the Rough

Our Home In Heaven

You've been in Heaven for ten years now
And our son has come to greet you
You weren't surprised by his arrival
Because somehow you already knew!

I'll bet you're having the time of your life
There with our only son
So many things to see in paradise
And praising the Holy One!

I can't wait to come there someday
And see my Heavenly Father first
I get so excited thinking about it
I feel my heart just wants to burst!

Then I will see the both of you
So peaceful and pain free
I wish I could have seen your faces
Knowing you were there through Eternity!

I know I'll have to wait a little longer
Only if it's God's plan
Sometimes I'm ready to go
Ready to be in the Promise Land!

Take care of you both until I get there
Oh, what a Glorious Day
I will be so filled with joy
Knowing with God, we'll always stay!

Diamonds in the Rough

He Has Made Me Strong

I keep seeing images in my mind
Of my son and what happened that day
I don't want to see them anymore
I pray that God will take them away!

My son's ashes sit in my closet
I can't believe that's him in there
One day when we're at the beach
We will scatter them everywhere!

I have his dad's ashes too
They've been sitting on the shelf for years
I can't bring myself to scatter them
I just want to keep them here!

Tragedies like this are so very painful
I didn't think in a million years
That my son would go before me
He went away and left me here!

I try not to think about that day
The words keep playing in my mind
When he told me that he had passed away
Relief I just needed to find!

It's so hard to lose a precious child
That you had raised for years
I know my son won't be coming back
And that really brings me to tears!

Diamonds in the Rough

The Lord is my comforter
He's been with me all along
And He will never leave me
And He has made me Stronger

Diamonds in the Rough

He Carries Me

God tells me if I trust Him
He will lead the way
Through this pain and heartache
He's here each and every day!

I've never really doubted Him
Because God's truth is on my mind
I know what He's promised me
That is peace and joy I'll find!

My loss is really got me down
I long to hold my son just once more
And a chance to say how much I love him
I just wonder what God has in store!

The Lords promises to me are set in stone
There can be no other way
He's promised to walk with me through the fire
Each and every day!

He carries me when I can't walk
Just like He said He would do
If you just trust Him now
He will surely carry you!

The Lord has been my shepherd
He's differently carried me
He's the best I've ever seen

Diamonds in the Rough

Peace And Joy He's Brought

The Lord doesn't promise a life without pain
The sun won't shine everyday
There will be days of darkness
Sometimes you'll feel like it will stay!

Whether you believe in a sovereign God
He still loves you anyway
When He whispers in a gentle voice
He wants you to open up and pray!

I've prayed more in this last year
Then I ever have before
Thinking of my son that's gone
Of my baby boy that I bore!

God doesn't expect me to understand
Why my boy had to go
I just feel like my heart is broken
And I just loved him so!

Time could take some of the pain away
That I've heard before
I know God has a plan for me
I long to know what He has in store!

I've excepted what has happened
Although this grief has broken my heart
God promises to get me through
Some peace and joy He has brought!

Diamonds in the Rough

God Is Here

As I viewed you for the very last time
You just laying there didn't seem real
I realized then, the pain I'd go through
So much before I could heal!

My legs were weak, my stomach was sick
Tears were rolling down my eyes
I really wasn't giving much time
To lean over and kiss you goodbye!

But I managed to do that
As I said, goodbye my son
I really didn't blame you at all
Because of what you'd done!

Your life was one of sadness
And all that I wanted for you
Is for you to have peace and happiness
And trust God in all you do!

We played a favorite song of yours
At your memorial service that day
Although I hadn't heard that song before
Now I cry when that song is played!

The Lord is very close to me
I can feel His presence each day
He's the reason that I survive
I wouldn't want it any other way!

Diamonds in the Rough

This Mountain

This mountain of pain is the highest
That I've ever seen before
I think that I have almost reached the top
But then I realize that there's much more!

I've climbed many mountains in my life
Some small and some rather high
I pray the Lord will help me climb this one together
I need Him to help me get by!

I never thought there was a mountain this steep
Until I lost my precious son
I've climbed it as high as I can right now
But there will be a long time before this is done!

I'll just take what life gives to me
Because I know the Lord will be right here
I want to fight with everything I have
But at times I want to disappear!

I want to climb this mountain top
But I just can't do it alone
So that's where Gods strength comes in
He sees my pain and hears me moan!

I know in time I'll get to the top
And I'll be on my way
To rid myself of this suffering and heartache
So peaceful I will be one day!

Diamonds in the Rough

God Took His Pain Away

I will never blame God for this tragedy
Even though it has shattered my heart
My son was so ready to go
Peace and joy all his life, he'd sought!

I just watched him over the years
And the unhappiness that he had
Knowing there was no way to help him
It just made me so very sad!

There are some that don't believe in a mental illness
They don't think depression is a big deal
They don't have a clue what it's like
To try to get your mind to heal!

They're people that think it's something you can snap out of
That you have a weakness inside
So many feel somewhat ashamed
And their feelings they try to hide!

I know my son was suffering
I could see the pain in his eyes
He just wanted to defeat this illness
For so many years He tried!

God was the only answer
And he asked Him to take his pain away
God knew when he allowed him to go
My son would be in Heaven with Him that day!

Diamonds in the Rough

This Grief Won't Keep Me Down

There are people that don't want God in my poems
But I'm going to keep writing them
He's the one that is getting me through
So I will keep writing for Him!

The Lord has been here for me so much
He's here to help me get by
Although the loss of my child is devastating
I haven't really asked God, why?

I do have some questions for Him
Things I've been thinking about so long
Like how am I getting through this grief
How have you made me this strong?

I am thankful that God has given me a gift
He tells me to share it with others
As I write these poems about grief
I'm happy to bring comfort to you mothers!

This pain I feel is heavy
But I won't let it keep me down
My time on this Earth will end someday
And I will be Heaven bound!

In Heaven to see my husband and son
I'm sure they've been waiting for me
Asking God to bring me home
So peaceful I can be!

Diamonds in the Rough

Only the Lord Understands

I really don't like Saturdays anymore
Because that's the day you passed away
It's just so sad what happened
I just wished that you could have stayed!

This pain and heartache just lingers on
I don't think it's going anywhere
I ask the Lord to take it away
But He says, your suffering I'll help you bear!

I just keep thinking about that day
That my heart and soul were shattered into
The moment I heard that you were gone
In my heart I already knew!

All his life was about suffering
And I just couldn't figure it out
Why he was even put on this Earth
But the answer I don't know about!

God will surely show me someday
The plan He had for everyone
Because I'll never figure it out by myself
Why this happened to my son!

I just know that I can always trust the Lord
With things I can never understand
One day He will make everything clear
He holds my son now in His hands!

Diamonds in the Rough

Our Pain Is Everyday

Somedays I miss you so very much
The pain in my heart is rough
God must know I can handle it
The past tragedies have made me tough!

The suffering in my past has made me strong
It's prepared me for this day
The day that I lost my only son
The heartache never goes away!

I know I couldn't do this on my own
So I call out to God when it gets bad
He's here to help get me through
And He knows this heartache makes me sad!

I find myself hiding my feelings
In front of people, I don't cry
Because I feel they're wanting me to finish grieving
So I just look at them and sigh!

They really don't know what we go through
They can't feel the pain in our hearts
They have children that are living
And our children have to be far apart!

I don't expect people to know our grief
But they don't have to stay away
Sometimes I just wish they would sit with me
Because this pain we face each day!

Diamonds in the Rough

I'll See Them Again

As I laid my husband and son to rest
It just felt like is wasn't true
This tragedy is so heartbreaking
I didn't know about what to do!

God knew exactly what I was going through
Suffering and pain so hard to bear
I've never had this much sorrow
My only hope now was prayer!

I just went to the Lord and just let it go
I've never felt such heartache before
I couldn't believe this was happening
This was my baby boy that I bore!

I don't know how long this grief will last
It could last for years
But I know I won't have to suffer alone
God sees my pain and tears !

I haven't ask Him why this happened
I think it was the only way
I know his life was miserable
So he decided he couldn't stay!

He's so peaceful right now
And my husband too
I can't wait to see them again
Hugging them is what I'll do!

Diamonds in the Rough

He'll Call Me Home

When God someday calls me home
How joyful I will be
No more pain or heartache
And my family I'll finally see!

I have been on a long journey
The worst I've ever known
But God has been so faithful
That He'll never leave me alone!

Losing a child is devastating
For I have lost my son
A pain inside like I've never known
My son's life on this Earth is done!

I just can't believe that it happened
And that this grief would be so bad
I really try to push forward
But the heartbreak I feel is sad!

I don't know about others, but I count on the Lord
He promises to get me through
He knows my spirit is wounded
And He knows exactly what to do!

I'm going to leave my pain and suffering with Him
And He'll wipe my tears away
I always feel His love for me
Each and every day!

Diamonds in the Rough

God's With Us To Stay

Some may think that God is to blame
When hardships come to them
But that I know is not true
We are loved so much by Him!

He sees every tear that we cry
And the deep pain in our heart
He knows the suffering and anguish
Our children have gone and we're far apart!

If we pray, God will come to us
He knows just how we feel
It might seem like this grief is lasting too long
But our hearts He wants to heal!

Our loss has been a journey
And I know the Lord can get us through
Even before He created us
Our lives He already knew!

He says there will be trials and tribulations
Some can be pretty tough
They're ones that have more then others
God knows when we've had enough!

The Lord won't leave us to grieve alone
He's with us night and day
We might not feel His presence
But He's truly with us to stay!

Diamonds in the Rough

I'll See My Son Again

I can't wait to see my son
He's walking streets of gold
He's in a place God promised
His body I want to hold!

God's given him a Glorious body
And wiped away his pain in tears
And sometimes when I'm really missing him
I wish he could be right here!

If he could come back just for a day
His new home he would tell me about
I've never questioned about Heaven
I know he's there without a doubt!

God says, come unto me when you're burdened
And He will give us rest
He's proven Himself to me many times
His love for us is the best!

I know my sufferings will be no more
When Heaven's gate I will walk through
The Lord will be there waiting for me
And He also be waiting for you!

I get excited knowing what my Eternity holds
And that I'll be there forever
So much time with my family
And we'll always be together!

Diamonds in the Rough

Our Children Are Peaceful

When you're sad and feel down
And you're heart feels like it is torn
Losing your child is so overwhelming
You've loved them since the day that he was born!

Think about their eternal home
How happy that they must be
God has called our children to Heaven
And one day we will see!

We'll see them like we never have
So peaceful and no more tears
For the Lord has wiped them away
Our children He does hold dear!

They're spending time with their family
And time will never end
God has promised us Eternity
A better place then where we've been!

They're there now walking streets of gold
And the light is never dim
The Lord is all the light we need
We will be there praising Him

I know someday we will be there
And my son I will embrace
Just knowing the Lord loves us so much
I can't wait until I see His face!

Diamonds in the Rough

Looking Forward To Heaven

I'm looking forward to Heaven
Where my husband and son will be
I just can't imagine the beauty there
At last I'll get to see!

My son finally will have his peace
Like he's never had before
I just don't know what we'll do there
I wonder what God will have in store!

I taught my children about this place
Where they'll never be pain are tears
The Lord will just wipe them away
And no more suffering or fear!

When I think about my loved ones there
My sadness turns to joy
And I would give anything
If I could just see my boy!

I know what Gods promises are
And I know He loves us very much
One day I see Him face to face
And He'll heal me with just a touch!

He knows what I'm going through
He's been here all along
And He's promised to bring me through
And helps me to be strong!

Diamonds in the Rough

A Home In Heaven

God led my son into Heaven
And he's experiencing peace and love
He brings I bet my boy is sitting beside the Lord
And just listening to the Angles sing!

When I think about my son
I have a smile on my face
Knowing he's in Heaven
Such a wonderful place!

I know it will be awhile before I see him
I feel God will keep me here
And follow along with His plan
So often I feel Him near!

I just can't imagine a place like Heaven
It seems too good to be true
But that's a promise from the Lord
Praising Him is what we'll do!

I just can't comprehend
That we'll spend Eternity there
God will wipe our tears away
So suffering we won't have to bear!

I really can't Thank Him enough
For all the things He does for me
He's going to share His home in Heaven
And all my loved ones there, I'll see!

Diamonds in the Rough

Safely To The End

I know your world is turning upside down
And the nightmares, they come and go
Waking up, you feel anxious and scared
This pain is all you know!

The pain that's been with you all along
You long to bid it, farewell
It's the worst you've ever seen
You pray it will leave right now!

You feel like your mind is out in the sea
Fighting the capsizing waves
You don't know if you can handle this storm
But, you can, you must be brave!

When the storms come they're powerful
You're trying to make it to the other side
It's the hardest thing you've ever done
And with all your might you've tried!

I've been through quite afew storms
And sometimes they knock me down
I fight back with all my might
Still feeling like I'm going to drown!

There's only one I can count on
That's the Lord, my best friend
I depend on Him to get me through
Safely to the end!

Diamonds in the Rough

I Will Comfort You

My heart right now just aches for him
My first and only son
I pray this grief I'm carrying
Would just leave me now, be done!

For I know that's not going to happen
I just might have years to go
The way I'm feeling this moment
The Lord is the only one that knows!

He will heal me in His time
And He'll always be beside me
He sees my pain and tears
Peaceful He wants me to be!

He is the one that can give me that peace
He has promised that before
His Holy Word, there's that promise
I've read it many times before!

I trust the Lord with all my heart
I have for many years
And I know He's not ready to take me
For some reason He wants me here!

I believe He has called me to serve others
And I think this feeling is true
To comfort someone in their grief
My desire is to help you!

Diamonds in the Rough

God's Plans

I know some people don't understand
Why God calls their children away
I've never questioned Him because I know
He'll show me someday!

We know it's not fair, and it's not
That our precious child, we have to lose
Some so young, and full of life
Inside our heart is bruised!

I questioned God when my husband passed
I told Him, it wasn't right
That he should be taken from us
And leave me crying day and night!

But the Lord knows more than I do
And He doesn't expect me to know His plan
So He took my husband peacefully
And He has him in His hands!

I know one day, the answers will unfold
And we will understand Gods will
Then He'll wipe our tears away
And we will then be healed!

I know that might not help right now
But I'm trusting in the Lord with my heart
And I know someday I'll be with my family
Never having to be apart!

Diamonds in the Rough

A Glorious Day

This loss has been the deepest pain
That I have ever known
Sometimes I want to be comforted
Other times I want to be all alone!

A detective came up that morning
He said my son had passed away
There was only one thing I could do
That's get on my knees and pray!

I was in shock that moment
I didn't think I was hearing him right
He gave me his card and left
And I saw him drive out of sight!

I set by the window here
And stared out, just in a daze
I knew your life wouldn't be too long
And I knew you would go that way!

I was out of it, not thinking clear
There were people coming in and out
I wondered if I would stay like this
This kind of grief, I knew nothing about!

This pain was deeper than my husband's
Although his was painful too
If it weren't for the Lord above
I don't know what I would do!

Diamonds in the Rough

My pain has gotten a little better
But it will never completely go away
I look forward to seeing them again
It will be a Glorious day!

Diamonds in the Rough

I Long To See My Boy

It's been awhile since my boy left
Because he just couldn't stay
He had fought this miserable illness
And he didn't think there was any other way!

I just wanted to save him
But that was something I just couldn't do
I didn't know the depth of his pain
Only the good Lord knew!

So He decided to answer his many prayers
And take him home where he was pain free
I just long to hold him so tight
I know one day with him, I'll be!

I can't make some people understand
How this grief at times brings me down
I just want to have someone here for me
And they don't have to utter a sound!

I just want to feel that they're bringing me comfort
And be with me when I'm sad
Because I lost my firstborn son
And I miss all the times we had!

I'll just carry on like I've been doing
And I know the Lord is my best friend
Sometimes He answers my prayers for me
And He know exactly where I've been!

Diamonds in the Rough

You're Happy And Peaceful

I'm really missing my boy so much
As time passes, I miss him more
Sometimes he's on my mind so much
I think any minute he'll walk through that door!

I'm sitting here crying and no one's around
I just feel so all alone
This pain I feel is so harsh
My broken heart just moans!

God comes to my rescue and tells me
That my boy will never suffer anymore
He's wiped his pain and tears away
And he's much happier then ever before!

I really believe that it is true
But when he left I died inside
I'm crying as much as before
But my pain I try to hide!

Some people can't understand
What we mothers go through
A heartache that we've never felt
Son, I'm broken because of you!

I'm not here to blame you
Because I know you were ready to go
I know now you're in perfect peace
I just love and miss you so!

Diamonds in the Rough

Forever More

Although I'm living here now
A part of me just died
The day that God took you home
And so many tears I've cried!

I know my life here won't last forever
Then I'll be in Heaven with you, son
I can't wait until that day comes
When my work in this life is done!

I try so hard to hold it together
But that's really difficult somedays
So I just pray to God for his help
I know no other way!

He'll walk with me through the fire
And carry me when He needs to
He'll wipe these tears I cry
His promises are so true!

I've kept the Lord pretty busy
In this last year or so
I know He stays right by my side
Everywhere I go!

So, I just need to focus on my life right now
Find out what God has in store
So, son I'll be there before you know it
And we'll be together for ever more!

Diamonds in the Rough

We're Going To Make It

We're going to make it, we're going to survive
Because that's what we mothers do
We hold our heads up because we're strong
And still we're grieving our babies too!

We really don't have a choice in the matter
We're left with this grief to bear
Day in and day out it goes
We're just living on a prayer!

A prayer that takes us through the storm
Through thunder and lightning and hail
Getting us to the other side
Now our ship is ready to sail!

God is my Captain through this journey
And I use His eyes to see
Whatever is coming towards me
I know He will set me free!

Sometimes things just happen
Things we just don't understand
But I feel safe knowing
That God holds me in His hands!

Diamonds in the Rough

Our Hearts Will Mend

I keep writing poems about you, son
Because you're always on my mind
I'm hoping they might help someone
Maybe peace inside they'll find!

So many of our children gone from us
We never thought in a million years
That we would be the ones living
In pain and wiping our tears!

This grief just slams us full force
It just takes our breath away
When I feel I can't take it any longer
I just go to the Lord and pray!

He gets me through like He promised
But I still feel much pain
I'm surprised after this trauma
My mind is intact and still sane!

At times it's so hard to breathe
Your heart's beating out of your chest
You just wish something would give
And give your mind some rest!

We have to hang in here together
This war we're going to win
It's just a matter of time
Before our hearts will start to mend!

Diamonds in the Rough

You're In Heaven Now

People wonder why you're not here
Why you had to go like you did
These people didn't know you
Because your pain and misery you hid!

Around your friends you smiled
Like there was nothing wrong
But you and I knew different
You had suffered for so long!

Why this illness, why so hard?
Through your life, it followed you
Never giving you a break
What it was doing, I surely knew!

I thought God would take your pain away
Because He always knows best
You just needed some assurance
And to give your mind some rest!

I felt helpless I couldn't help you
I saw you struggle for years
It was just out of my hands
I often saw you in tears!

I'm sorry your life wasn't normal
I wanted so much for you
But I know that you're in Heaven now
And there are lots of things to do!

Diamonds in the Rough

If You Knew

If you knew how much I adored you, son
If you knew how much I cared
Then you'd never have a question
Of why, this pain I bear!

If you knew the year you started school
Made me really sad
And I cried all week long
About all the time together we had!

If you knew how bad I felt
When you got in trouble at school
I tried to guide you the right way
But you just couldn't follow the rules!

If you knew how heartbroken it made me feel
When I saw sadness in your eyes
This mental illness wouldn't budge
No matter how hard we tried!

If you knew how crushed it made me feel
When you said you didn't want to live anymore
I just talked to you through the night
This had happened other times before!

If you knew how devastating that it felt
When I learned that you were gone
Your life flashed before my eyes
And I thought of our special bond!

Diamonds in the Rough

If you only knew how peaceful
I feel Because in Heaven the Lord has you
Never to have to suffer again
Your pain and tears are wiped away too!

Diamonds in the Rough

Quite A Boy

I rocked my baby boy at night
His little body I loved to hold
I watched him as he took each breath
I felt comfort in my soul!

I loved him more than life itself
Thankful God had given him to me
A few years went by and he grew older
Some changing I could see!

I saw him run the bases in little league
And saw him hit his first ball
He glanced at me with that smile
That was the best moment of all!

Time moved on and he was growing
Before I knew it, he was a teen
Primping in front of the mirror
The most handsome boy, I'd ever seen!

We spent lots of time together
And he taught me a thing or two
He looked forward to his future
Alot of things he wanted to do!

I found out what it was like to raise a son
He brought me so much joy
I was especially proud of him
He was quite a boy!

Diamonds in the Rough

Now he's gone to a peaceful place
And I miss him with all my heart
When I think of him, I always remember
Much happiness to me he brought!

Diamonds in the Rough

The Lord Knows

It's so sad to hear your child tell you
That he hates his life and wants to die
It really wasn't a surprise to me
Because all of these years, I've known why!

Years of mental illness
Since he was just a boy
Monsters taking away his happiness
Inside, stealing his joy!

Not having all the answers
Just not knowing what to do
So I prayed to God and talked to Him
About what He already knew!

Some things in life are so unfair
But I was taught not to question why?
That the Lord holds all the answers
And He'll give us the strength to get by!

I have felt His strength many times
All through the years
But when it gets to be too much
Here come the pain and tears!

I won't question the Lord about my son
And why he had to go
Because I know he's at peace
But I still love and miss him so!

Diamonds in the Rough

I'm In His Arms

I asked the Lord how long will this last
This pain and heartache too
He answers me in a gentle voice
And says, I'll make a way for you

He says that He's been with me all along
At times I couldn't feel Him though
I was so deeply into my sorrow
He was there but, I just didn't know!

He's seen every tear that I've ever cried
And He knows me inside and out
I know that He's always loved me
And this, I have no doubt!

Why He's allowed this suffering
Only He knows why
In time He will tell me
And wipe the tears from my eyes!

Losing a child is devastating
It's a pain that you don't get use to
The Lord just takes me under His arms
Trusting Him is all I can do!

I miss my son so very much
More as time has passed
I hope the love I have for him
Will be enough to last!

Diamonds in the Rough

I'll Meet Them At The Gate

My husband has been gone for awhile now
And I still love and miss him too
It took me by surprise when he left
I didn't know what to do!

He and our son are there in Heaven together
I'm sure they had some catching up to do
I didn't know that they would be leaving
The Lord is the only one who knew!

I know now that they are safe
There isn't a better place to be
Surrounded by Gods love
It just brings joy to me!

It's been so hard on me
And to get through each day
Feeling so all alone here
But I know God will make a way!

Much pain and heartache I have known
That I shouldn't of had to go through
But I try to just accept it
Because I love my family, it's true!

I count on seeing them again
And with open arms, I'll run
To meet them at the beautiful gate
My husband and my son!

Diamonds in the Rough

If I Could Have One Wish

My heart and soul have been crushed into
Like I have never known before
I just wonder what God is doing
And what He has in store!

I've had many trials and tribulations
Down through the years
But this has been the worst
And I've shed so many tears!

I know that the Lord has helped me
I feel it everyday
I know that He is the only one
That can take my pain away!

This grief hasn't been easy
It has been difficult losing my child
But I know I'll see him again
Maybe in a little while!

If I could have one wish
With my son is where I'd be
He'd tell me about Gods wonderful place
So joyful it would be to me!

I don't know how much time is left
Before the Lord calls me there
For now I'm dealing with the pain and tears
That one day, I won't have to bear!

Diamonds in the Rough

I'd Climb The Highest Mountain

I would climb the highest mountain
And sail the stormy seas
To get to Heaven and tell you
How much you mean to me!

You left your place in this world
And I have been so sad
Thinking about when you were a boy
And the fun times we had!

We'd go to the beach as a family
And see the water, the sun, and the sand
You were just a little guy then
So you had to take your daddy's hand!

We would play for hours
Until we were all worn out
It was nice spending time together
That's what family is all about!

You've been gone for some time now
I only wish I could see your smile
I look forward to seeing you again
But it might not be for awhile!

I loved you so much and I still do
You were the apple of my eye
I was proud to have you as my son
I'm trying hard to get by!

Diamonds in the Rough

I ask the Lord for help everyday
He's the reason that I get through
I just have a longing to see you again
I love and really miss you to!

Diamonds in the Rough

Reunited We'll Be

I asked the Lord sincerely one day
To not let my children go before me
It would be such a tragedy
So brokenhearted I'd be!

The very thing that brought anxiety to me
The thing I worried the most about
Has happened now and I am crushed
I trusted God and I didn't have a doubt!

I know that His ways are not ours
And He has our best interest at heart
But It's so hard to live without my son
Wondering why we have to be apart!

I really don't blame the Lord for his passing
I just accept it but, it's hard to do
God has watched over him through his life
So, what happened is what He already knew!

People tell me that I am strong
I've had to be through the years
I've been through alot, more than my share
So much pain and tears!

God will one day explain things to me
That right now I don't understand
Like why He saw fit to take my boy
And how He has him in His hands!

Diamonds in the Rough

I'm really looking forward to that day
When once again my son I'll see
I'll hug him like I never have
And he'll be reunited with me!

Diamonds in the Rough

Our Broken Hearts

What do we do when our heart is beyond broken?
And the tears in our eyes flow free
This road we're on is long and hard
It just takes the wind out of me!

Others will never feel what we do
Unless they have walked our road
They don't know we have to be strong
To carry this heavy load!

Pain and suffering like we've never known
We don't know how we're getting through
I know someone that I count on
His love for me is true!

I never thought I could handle this pain
I didn't think I was strong enough
But I've learned over this year
That I must be pretty tough!

The Lord knows what I can handle
Over the years I've suffered so much
By my side He's always been
To heal me with His loving touch!

This tribulation has been so painful
I try to make it through each day
I won't stop fighting it
No matter how long it stays!

Diamonds in the Rough

In My Heart To Stay

Where is time going these days
It seems like only yesterday
That I rocked you in my arms
And longed for you to stay!

I held my sons hand for a little while
And then I held him in my heart
I couldn't believe that he was mine
Much love and joy he brought!

He grew up so fast back then
Where had my little boy gone?
We had such good times together
And we had that special bond!

I didn't want him to grow up and leave home
But I knew it would happen one day
I just wanted him to stay my little boy
And I wish there were a different way!

Tragedies happen and we don't know why
It's just so hard to figure out
All our pain and suffering
It shouldn't be what life is about!

So, I just keep my son safely in my heart
That's where he's going to stay
The Lord has promised that we'll meet again
I look so forward to that day!

Diamonds in the Rough

The Dream

My son came to me in a dream one night
I could see the peacefulness on his face
He said he was sorry that he had to leave
But he needed to go to a better place!

I didn't need any apologies
Because I knew just how he felt
I also suffered from this illness
So I know what this pain is about!

I was so happy to see him
That I wished this dream would last forever
Just holding him in my arms
And spending much time together!

I realize that it was his time to go
But it still breaks my heart so bad
To live the rest of my life without him
Just makes me really sad!

I hope as time passes on
My heart will start to heal
But there's a chance it will last a long time
That's just the way I feel!

I said goodbye to him in the dream
I wish I didn't have to go
But God promises I'll see him again
I just love and miss my son, so!

Diamonds in the Rough

My Poems I Write

I write a lot of poems about grief
But my friend tells me it's time to move on
She's says to write something more cheerful
She doesn't know that I still morn!

I can't just forget about my son
He was my pride and joy
I guess I'll always write about him
Because he was my special boy!

I don't expect people to understand
Because they really don't have a clue
What it's like to lose a child
The pain we feel, me and you!

He's on my mind all of the time
And the waves of grief just come
I just wonder how long it will last
I just wish it would ease up some!

Most people don't know the pain we're in
And I pray they never do
It's the worst agony I've ever felt
Because my love for my son was true!

I might decide to write cheerful poems later
But for now, it's not inside me
I need to write my feelings down
So other people can see!

Diamonds in the Rough

They'll see and maybe feel comfort
More they can do on their own
Through prayer I let God in
So I'll never have to be alone!

Diamonds in the Rough

They're Healed By The Masters Touch

How long will our grief last
It's not something we want to do alone
My body just feels so heavy
I feel I'm weighed down with stones!

Sometimes it's just hard to move
And your chest is feeling so tight
You're giving it all you have
Pushing through with all your might!

I have images in my mind
That never go away
I've asked the Lord to remove them
So I can be free of them one day!

It's so hard on all of us
To get through this tragedy
I'm fighting with everything I have
I asked God to rescue me!

He comes to me in a gentle voice
And I feel a peacefulness flood my soul
He knows exactly what I'm going through
And He knows my son, I just want to hold!

It's been a year and I'm still brokenhearted
And I miss him so very much
But I know my son's with Jesus
His pain has been healed by the Master's touch!

Diamonds in the Rough

A Chance To Heal

Some of my poems aren't really about religion
But about the Lord that's always here
I count on Him tremendously
To get me through the pain and tears!

I really wouldn't know how to handle it
If I had to deal with this grief alone
But I feel that He is taking care of me
And His love, I've always known!

I long for others to feel the peace God gives
After a tragedy, when your heart is broken into
Through all of this you don't understand
You don't know what you're supposed to do!

That's where God comes in, to help you
Sometimes He's all that I can see
When this suffering goes on and on
I know that He's right beside me!

I'm so glad I have this group right now
Because the pain and heartache feel so real
It gives me the chance to help others
And maybe give their heart a chance to heal!

Diamonds in the Rough

With Me God Will Always Be

These waves of pain come and go
I don't know when they will end
I can't let anyone in on it
I just can only pretend!

I've never felt heartache quite like this
It just reaches down into your soul
I really want to scream and holler
And my child I want to hold!

We know our children aren't coming back
No matter how much we want them to
We know they're happy and at peace
Finding comfort is all we can do!

The Lord has brought me that comfort
But it's still really tough
You don't know how you're going to make it
You tell God that you've had enough!

He knows all about our pain
And when it will someday end
He's watched us through the years
And He knows where we have been!

I will continue to trust the Lord
No matter what life brings to me
I'm not afraid to face heartbreak
Because with me, God will always be!

Diamonds in the Rough

In My Heart He Stays

While I'm going through this difficult trial
In Gods arms is where I'll be
He loves me with an everlasting love
And He brings comfort to me!

He has really blessed me lately
When He answers my prayers
I tell Him that I count on Him
Because this pain is too much to bear!

As mothers, we're in this together
And losing our child, is going to take awhile
Our hearts are heavy and burdened
It's even a effort to get out a smile!

No one really understands
Unless they've walked down our road
They don't know the pain we're in
We're carrying a heavy load!

I've prayed so much this past year
And God is seeing me through
He promises never to leave us
He'll bring peace to me and you!

Somedays I feel like my old self
But that's few and far between
Other days I feel much heartache
It's the worst I've ever seen!

Diamonds in the Rough

So, I'm just counting on the Lord
To get me through each day
I love and miss my son so much
In my heart is where he stays!

Diamonds in the Rough

He Holds Me In His Arms

Life doesn't mean waiting until the storm is over
But learning to dance in the rain
No matter how strong the storm is
We have to try to get through the pain!

It will never be easy for us
We've loved our babies since they were born
We had a lot of dreams for them
But now our hearts are torn!

We wonder how we'll get through this
I just keep on pushing through
I don't know how long it will last
But, I really love and miss him too!

I'd never want my son to see me like this
Because it would break His heart
Although he knows that God is helping me
Much peace to me, He's brought!

Some people grieve differently
Only the good Lord knows
How much we can stand
He sees our highs and our lows!

I know with time this will get better
This misery and heartache in my soul
I know God is getting me through
And to me, in His arms, He does hold!

Diamonds in the Rough

Good Times We Had

So many memories I have of my son
I now keep them in my heart
Thinking back to some good times
And the joy to me, he brought!

There were times in his life that he was happy
And then times that he was sad
I think back to his childhood
And remember the fun we had!

Sometimes he was peculiar
He didn't want to plant flowers with me
Didn't want to get his hands dirty
A frown on his face I'd see!

I enjoyed having my little boy
I'd kiss him every night
Then he'd reach up and kiss me
And hug me with all his might!

We'd play ball and catch fireflies
Run through puddles and climb trees
He loved spending time with me
So happy he would be!

I miss those time that we had
I cherish them everyday
I feel peaceful that he's in Heaven
I wouldn't want it any other way!

Diamonds in the Rough

I Hold My Head High

Someday I'll look back at this grief
And I'll know that God got me through
I feel like I must be strong
To go through losing a son like you!

No one can know the pain we feel
Unless they've gone through it too
I wouldn't wish this on no one
Because this misery in my heart is true!

I'll try to hold my head up high
Even through the pain and tears
I don't expect the grief to be gone
Because it's only been a year!

It's really been a hard one, this year
At times I felt like I was falling apart
The Lord picks me up when I'm falling
And gives me peace in my heart!

I didn't realize that grieving would be so bad
I've been crying for over a year
I wonder how long it will go on
I just wish that my son were here!

But I know that he's in perfect peace
And God has him in his care
I know it may be years before I see him
But someday I will be there!

Diamonds in the Rough

We'll Get Through

This grief is hard but we'll get through
On the Lord, I do depend
He brings me through the pain and tears
And helps my heart to mend!

This pain feels worse than the day you left
It just sometimes doesn't feel real
But I'm not giving up, I'll just move along
Just hoping that someday I'll heal!

God must think I'm strong
To give me what I'm going through
It was always in the back of my mind
That one day, I might lose you!

I just wish you would have talked to me
And we would have figured it out
But I know you were afraid that I'd be hurt
If I knew what you were thinking about!

These waves of pain just come over me
Sometimes I don't know what to do
This is the worse grief that I've ever felt
I never thought I'd be losing you!

One day I'll be Heaven bound
It will be a day like none other
I love and miss you so much
And I'm proud that I was your mother!

Diamonds in the Rough

I'll See You In A Little While

I've written many poems for you
The words flow from my heart
We use to be so close
But now we're far apart!

I've tried to write different poems
But my mind just goes back to you
I guess it helps me with this grieving
Slows down my pain and tears too!

What I would give to see you again
Just for a little while
If I could just walk to Heaven
I'd walk a million miles!

I love you, son with all my heart
So sorry that you had to go
I had a feeling that you were leaving
But other things I didn't know!

We don't know all the answers
So I let the Lord figure it out
And someday He will show us
What His plan was about!

For now I'll let Him guide me
Through this tribulation and trial
Don't worry about me because I'll be fine
And I'll see you in a little while!

Diamonds in the Rough

I Thought The World Of You

I've been crying alot, all day long
I just can't believe it's true
That you're gone and not coming back
I'm just grieving so much for you!

I know that time is moving on
And it's been over a year
But that doesn't stop my love for you
Because I held you dear!

The tears, they come and they go
Soon they'll be wiped away
God promises that to us
I can't wait until that wonderful day!

You're there my son, so peaceful
Just like I knew you would be
I just can't get you out of my mind
Because I thought the world of you!

I know that I'll move along someday
And that God will get me through
He has helped me tremendously
Dealing with the loss of you!

Diamonds in the Rough

All That Matters

My next trip to the beach, you'll be with me
I'm spreading your ashes out to sea
Not all, but some of them
The rest I'll keep for me!

You wanted your ashes to be with your dads
So this wish, I'll grant you
I know it will be an upsetting moment
It will bring tears to my eyes too!

I haven't been to our favorite beach since you were thirteen
I remember the good times we had
I wished they could've lasted forever
With you, your sister and dad!

It's so hard to accept that half my family is gone
I wouldn't have thought it would happen that way
So here I'm left to heavily grieve
Sometimes everyday!

As the time moves on, I miss you so much
But I keep you in my heart to stay
If I could just see you one more time
There's so much I want to say!

I know the way you left, had been on your mind
For along time, many years
You just didn't have the courage back then
Even though the pain and tears!

Diamonds in the Rough

Well, I know where you are, and that's all that matters
The Lord has wiped those tears away
And He'll do the same for me
When I see Him on that Glorious day!

Diamonds in the Rough

For A Little While

God gave you to me for a little while
Because He knew you would bring me joy
Such joy like I've never felt
You were my precious boy!

You were a child, a teen and a young adult
We spent this time together
Although you're not here anymore
This will not last forever!

I hold your blanket close to my heart
That someone made for me
When I go away, I will take it
And think about the memories!

This life I live is passing fast
It really seems like that to me
So maybe it won't seem to long
Before your face I'll see!

The Lord had a good reason
For bringing you to Heaven that day
He knew of your sufferings here
And didn't want you to live that way!

Although it's really breaking my heart
The longer I go without you
It helps to know you're in perfect peace
And you're there with family too!

Diamonds in the Rough

I've Finally Made It Home

Mom, please don't worry about me
Because I finally made it home
There are so many sights to see here
So many places to roam!

When I first got here, I looked around
Because I wanted to see Jesus first
I was just so full of excitement
I thought I was just going to burst!

Well, I finally laid my eyes on Him
And then instantly I was at peace
I never, ever felt this before
And all my pain was released!

Then I searched around for my dad
I found him with a smile upon his face
He welcomed me home to be with him
He said I'd come to a beautiful place!

I saw many more family here
And they seemed happy as can be
They told me they were glad I'd come
Then they all came and hugged me!

I can't wait until you get here, mom
But I know that people are counting on you
So stay there a little longer
And someday you'll be here too!

Diamonds in the Rough

Releasing These Tears

Crying is for releasing tears
Because the Lord made us that way
I know it makes me feel better
Even if I cry everyday!

The tears just run down my face
God's counting every one
These tears continue to fall
Because I've lost my son!

I've never cried so much in my life
Then I have this past year
I don't know when they'll let up
I miss my son and hold him dear!

The tears are here in the morning
And sometimes during the night
I try to get through it
I push with all my might!

When people see me crying
They often ask me why
They don't have a clue to what
I'm going through I'm trying my best to get by!

All I need is comfort sometimes
It would really help me out
I know people can't understand
What this grief inside is about!

Diamonds in the Rough

You've Crossed Over

You haven't left son, you've just crossed over
Over to the Heavenly side
With everything so wonderful
With those pearly gates so wide!

There's no place better than where you are
You're in the presence of the King!
Just sitting there, getting to know Him
And listening to the Angels sing!

I have to say, I'm a little jealous
That you got there before me
But long ago it was reserved for you
Because Heavens where you've wanted to be!

I know it's not my turn yet
So, I'll have to wait awhile
I picture you, and when I do
You're just standing there with a smile!

A smile that tells me that you are happy
God's given you peace, thus far
And joy like you've never known
I'm just excited to know where you are!

I will be joining you someday
And, oh how I'll be enjoying the sights
When I see Jesus, I'll know
That everything will be alright!

Diamonds in the Rough

Your Dad And You

You told your sister to spread your ashes
Right along with your dads
At the beach, off the pier
I remember the good times you had!

Your dad helped you ride the waves
You both had so much fun
Building castles in the sand
And trying to catch some sun!

On the pier, lines thrown out
It was you and your dads favorite thing to do
Anticipating a really big catch
Somehow you just knew!

So, we ate your big fish for dinner that night
You were as proud as could be
You loved spending time with your dad
And that just tickled me!

I enjoyed watching you two together
You'd formed a bond over the years
Such a sweet man and his son
You both I held so dear!

Someday I'll go back to the beach
And I'll spread you two together
Then one day, I will join you
And we'll be in Heaven forever!

Diamonds in the Rough

I Adored Our Time Together

When you were first born, I held you
I knew you'd be a special boy
Thinking about the years to come
And how you would bring me so much joy!

The years went by like I thought they would
And I loved spending time with you
You always tried to please me
Bringing me flowers, is what you'd do!

I watched you climb trees and catch fireflies
And sometimes I'd help you too
Run through fields of flowers
I had fun just watching you!

You were excited about God's creation
I taught you about it when you were young
We talked about the moon and stars
How He made them before we had begun!

I thanked God for giving me a boy like you
More than I expected, much more
And for given me twenty-seven years
Our time together, I adored!

Diamonds in the Rough

God's Taking Care Of You

I had a feeling that you were leaving
And it made me feel so sad
I couldn't get these thoughts out of my mind
What I was feeling, was really bad!

I knew that you had given up
You just couldn't do this anymore
Anxiety and depression got the best of you
In your mind you were fighting a war!

Life was not what you thought it would be
No happiness or joy
I really hated to see you this way
You were my precious son, my boy!

God doesn't promise us life without sorrow
But He does promise to be here
To walk through the fire with us
And He sees our every tear!

I taught you son about Gods love
And how He can get you through
But things had gotten so bad
That only your suffering, God knew!

I have mixed feelings about what happened
And it just crushes my heart into
But I think it's much better
That God is now taking care of you!

Diamonds in the Rough

Dreams Of You

Sometimes I just need a break
To dry my eyes, full of tears
I want to feel you close now
And I just want to have you here!

I'm sure you're better where you are
There's no doubt in my mind
I told you about a future life
How peace and joy, you'd find!

Maybe I shouldn't wish for you to come back
I know you're as happy as can be
But, so many days I've cried for you
The pain has taken ahold of me!

Sometimes I ask the Lord to relieve me
To not let me cry so much
Then my mind feels more peaceful
I can feel His gentle touch!

At times I dream that we are together
It is my dream come true
I put my arms around you, and hold you tight
And remember the times I had with you!

You are my child, my only son
In my heart is where you'll stay
Until I get to that Glorious place
I can't wait until that day!

Diamonds in the Rough

A Glorious Place

Heaven is like nothing we've ever seen
And more wonderful than we'll ever know
God has created a paradise for us
It's because He loves us so!

I want to see the Lord first
And then my family
Some have been there a long time
Just waiting there for me!

I can't wait to step through those gates of pearl
And see the mansions gems
I know they'll be breathtaking
I'm just so thankful for Him!

The streets there will be of gold
And we'll wear robes pure white
There will be only Gods light
There will be no night!

We'll be led in by Angels I can't wait to hear them sing
We'll all be so perfect there
And feel the peace God brings!

All those that trust in Him
Will inherit this Glorious place
I want to feel His love for me
And look upon His face!

Diamonds in the Rough

How Happy I Will Be

Son, if you could know how much I love and miss you
If we could see each other face to face
Then I'd know how happy you are
Heaven is an awesome place!

I know you longed to go there
With everything in your heart
I just feel that you're at peace
But I hate for us to be apart!

I know how much you suffered
And how you didn't like your life here
I often saw you struggle
And your eyes were full of tears!

I felt like my hands were tied
I didn't know what to do
I just really wanted to see you well
And see joy on your face too!

Sometimes the days seem to never end
At the times that I'm crying for you
I know that the Lord is beside me
And I know that His promises are true!

He says that He'll carry me through
No matter the pain that I'm in
I can't believe it's been this long
Since this awful heartache began!

Diamonds in the Rough

I know that I'm going to be ok
I just don't know when that will be
I'm just looking forward to seeing you
So happy our reunion will make me!

Diamonds in the Rough

In Heaven Is Where I'll Be

I cry out to God to be by my side
To comfort me and wipe away my tears
It's been such a hard time for me
And I know it's gonna hurt for many years!

I do feel the Lord when He comes to me
And tells me that He can make me, brand new
I tell Him that it will be a long time
But that, He already knew!

These teardrops fall like a heavy rain
Wishing they would go away
I'm crying out for my son
I just wished that he could've stayed!

I wonder if he knows the misery I'm in
I don't know if God will let him see
There is no sadness in Heaven
Just peaceful everyone will be!

I know this pain may not last through my life
But I don't feel like that right now
This emotional turmoil on the inside
I wish I could fix it, but how?

I do depend on the Lord alot
But it still gets pretty bad
The worse time is when I'm alone
I think of the good times we had!

Diamonds in the Rough

I know I'll see my son again
God's promised that to me
And as I pass through the gates of Heaven
With my son is where I'll be!

Diamonds in the Rough

I Want Him Here

I'm sitting here crying my eyes out
Scared I'm going to lose control
I didn't know it would hurt this bad
Pain that digs deep into my soul!

I don't have anyone to call
No one to calm me down
I just wish it were time
For me to be Heaven bound!

I know the Lord doesn't want that
He has a plan for me
To carry out what His will is
But right now I just can't see!

I open my mouth to cry sometimes
And nothing really comes out
Just silence and misery
I'm really learning what grief is about!

I pray to God to stop me
From slowly losing my mind
I want to hear from my son
So I ask if He could give me a sign!

I don't want anyone to see me like this
Sometimes it's just a bad day
I never know when it's coming
Tomorrow I might be ok!

Diamonds in the Rough

I'm just thinking about my son so much
It's every night and day
Just trying to get him out of my mind
So this pain will go away!

It helps to know where he is
No more pain or tears
I know God loves him so much
But sometimes I just want him here!

Diamonds in the Rough

Your Pain And Tears Are Erased

I hold you close, in my heart
And that's where you will stay
Until that Glorious moment
When we meet again someday!

I will always treasure what we had
So many memories of you and I
We'd lay in the grass and watch
So many stars that were in the sky!

You were my Angel, my firstborn
A boy that I dreamed you would be
I remember holding you for the first time
What a beautiful moment for me!

I remember trying to make you happy
That's really I wanted for you
But something changed over the years
And I didn't know what to do!

Missing our time we once had
Because you just pulled away
I realized something was wrong
You seemed to be sad everyday!

I'm relieved that all that is over
And now you're in a better place
I know you're happy and at peace
And your pain and tears are erased!

Diamonds in the Rough

Someday I Will See

I never thought my heart would be broken
The way it has been in the last year
I can't believe that it is real
I go through much pain and tears!

I know I have to move on someday
But my heart won't let me go
My son is just on my mind so much
Because I love and miss him so!

I feel there are people that think it's time to heal
But I don't think that's true
There are people that don't understand
Oh, if they only knew!

If they could hear my heart and soul cry out
Then they would truly know
That this misery of grieving
Is a journey that's very slow!

There are people that don't talk about my son
But I would like them to
Because when I hear his name
It's obvious that I do!

I feel I've cried all of my tears out
And I don't want to cry anymore
I wish God would tell me
What He has in store!

Diamonds in the Rough

I feel something good will happen
From my ashes, there could be beauty
Only the Lord knows about it
One day maybe I'll see!

Diamonds in the Rough

Our Broken Hearts Will Be Healed

You're sitting there wondering
If your life will ever be good
This grief just goes on and on
And we're often misunderstood!

It's so difficult getting through it
Days, months and years
Still the grief is the same
We've cried so many tears!

They say that we'll get better
That someday we'll move on
They don't understand our love
We've had since the day our child was born!

I sit in your room, looking out the window
Just like you use to do
I'm thinking about the pain you suffered
And only the Lord really knew!

I'm not saying, I'd call you back
Even though this pain has been tough
I ask God to ease it up
Because I think I've had enough!

No one will ever know
The misery inside we feel
But I rest assured that someday
Our hearts that are broken will be healed!

Diamonds in the Rough

A Brighter Tomorrow

I don't think anyone notices the sadness in my eyes
Or sees my silent cry
I'm just thinking about that day
That I had to tell you goodbye!

It was a day like no other
And I was trying to be strong
I was there to bid you, farewell
Your death, I thought was so wrong!

It didn't have to happen
But I couldn't get through to you
There were ways to get help
But I don't think you knew!

This should never had happened
But there was only so much I could do
I tried to help you through the years
And you knew how much I loved you too.

So many sons and daughters leaving this way
It really makes me so sad
I wish someway I could reach them
So, they wouldn't have to leave the life they had!

We all need to pay attention
Because these people don't give us a clue
They're suffering through this illness alone
It's all that they can do!

Diamonds in the Rough

They just want someone to listen
To share in their pain and sorrow
To give them a positive outlook
So maybe they can have a better tomorrow!

Diamonds in the Rough

I Hold You In My Heart

I'm waiting for my Doctor
Sitting in this chair here
You are strongly on my mind
I close my eyes and shed a tear!

I hold you in my heart now
That's the only place you can be
Until my life is finished
And then your face, I'll see!

I'm looking so forward to that day
When this pain will be no more
I'll wrap my arms around you
Just like I did before!

It will be different this time
Because it will be a Heavenly place
And I can't wait to meet my Savior
Just to look upon His face!

The days and months go by so fast
But this pain slows my mind down
Just hoping I could see you now
I would love having you around!

I know that day will come
But I know the Lord needs me here
To follow out His plan for me
For to Him I am dear!

Diamonds in the Rough

My Life Won't Fade

I've been around for quite a few years
And I'm not going to let my life go
Even though there's been much heartache
Because I lost my son, that I love so!

Since this has happened to me
I just want to see His face
To see the wonderful joy he holds
And know he's in a better place!

He's on my mind so much
I hope the pain gets better someday
I know I'll get through this
Because I go to God and pray!

I've never really asked why
When tragedies happen to me
I bear it the best I can
But sometimes sad, I'll be!

I know this pain will last awhile
But I know that I am strong
And I know that you're in Heaven with the Angels
Joyfully singing beautiful songs!

I won't let my life fade away
So I can be in Heaven with you
I know the Lord I can depend on
And I know He'll get me through!

Diamonds in the Rough

Your Beautiful Tree

I planted a cherry blossom tree
In memory of you
I planted it a year ago
It's what I chose to do!

I go there and talk to you
And I feel that you are near
Sometimes I think I hear your voice
But I realize that you're not here!

I've placed things you like around the tree
Like cats and cardinals and such
It sometimes makes me cry
Because I love and miss you so much!

I ask the Lord to protect your tree
To let it grow strong and tall
And when it's grown someday
It will be the most beautiful of all!

I try not to be sad too much
Because I know that you're with your dad
I sure do miss my husband
And all the good times we had!

I know you're both with the Lord
And someday I'll be there too
I'll always remember the memories, son
That I keep in my heart for you!

Diamonds in the Rough

I Hold Him Dear

This broken heart should never be
We feel broken beyond repair
This pain is really breaking us apart
It feels it's too much to bear!

I think of my son constantly
He's always on my mind
I know if I turn it over to God
Peace I'll one day find!

We can't believe this has happened
Life has taken our child away
And as much as it hurts right now
We'll be with them again someday!

Hope is embedded in our souls
That we can move through these tragedies
Someday our pain will lessen
And maybe happy, we'll be!

I've never expected life without sorrow
Trials and tribulations we'll bear
But remembering God's promise
I go to Him in prayer!

He helped me through like I never imagined
And He's true to His word
When I draw close to Him
His gentle voice I think I've heard!

Diamonds in the Rough

He tells me that He sees my brokenness
And He's been watching me this last year
He promises to reunite with me
My son that I hold dear!

Diamonds in the Rough

Someday I Will Know

I looked into your eyes that day
And there wasn't a sparkle there
I didn't know that you'd be going
Because your life was too much to bear!

I didn't say , I love you
But I hugged you really tight
A sadness came over me
As you drove out of sight!

The night of the tragedy
I thought I would have woken up and known
That maybe you were in danger
I just know you were all alone!

I know you were in great anguish
I wish I could've been with you
The Lord saw what was happening
He was the only one that knew!

I know you're in Heaven now
Because the Lord told me so
I can't find the answers to my questions
But someday I will know!

Diamonds in the Rough

You're In My Heart

You passed away on a Saturday
That's when I got the news
You'd been missing for a few days
I couldn't believe that this was true!

Not knowing where you were
I didn't sense anything was wrong
Although I worried for your safety
But I knew I had to be strong!

The detective told me they had found you
You had walked the road all night
Maybe trying to make up your mind
If you wanted to continue with this fight?

I'm sorry that it came to this
I just couldn't believe my ears
When I realized that you were gone
I fought through the pain and tears!

Now you're home with the Lord
It's where you wanted to go
Your pain and suffering, you hid from me
I really didn't know!

One day this pain will lessen
But I'll still keep you in my heart
And someday when I see you
Then, we'll never be apart!

Diamonds in the Rough

God Stays By My Side

You're in much pain and suffering
Your hearts been broken in two
You can't believe your son is gone
This tragedy can't be true!

Some time has gone by since it happened
And you still don't understand why
He loved life and seemed happy
Why would he want to die?

You thought you knew him inside and out
But you didn't have a clue
The pain that was in his heart
The misery that he hid from you!

Now you're left with questions
They won't be answered, you know
You're doubting that you'll move on
Because you love and miss him so!

I have been down and broken too
Like I've never been before
I ask the Lord to help me through
Because I can't take it anymore!

So, He comes through for me
And He promises that He'll stay
Right along beside me
Each and everyday!

Diamonds in the Rough

Missing You

Ten years today, you went to be with the Lord
And I miss you so much, my love!
Time has gone by so fast
You're resting in Heaven above!

I never knew you would be leaving
It really took me by surprise
I didn't know you wouldn't be coming home
Didn't know I'd have to say goodbye!

All these years have gone by
And there's an aching in my heart
Just really longing for you
It feels so sad that we're apart!

The Lord has truly gotten me through
There's been years of pain and tears
I know I'll see you again someday
I love and hold you dear!

You were a good husband and father
Like a queen, you treated me
I'll always be grateful to you
And someday together, we'll be!

Diamonds in the Rough

It's Ok To Cry

You're letting your pain and emotions out
So crying doesn't mean you're not strong
The tears actually release your pain
So, know that crying is never wrong!

The Lord knows what our tears are for
And He's bottling up each one
When we get to Heaven, we'll see
That there's been alot of crying done!

At times in life, things hurt so bad
You don't think you'll make it through
I know those feelings so well
That's why crying is what you should do!

I've hurt this past year like never before
Because I've lost my son
Many tears have welled up in my eyes
So, much crying is what I've done!

I don't like to cry except when I'm alone
And only God sees me then
He comes along and softens the blow
In Him I can always depend!

When I see someone crying
I always ask if they're ok
I'll sit with them for awhile
And try to brighten their day!

Diamonds in the Rough

Many People Are Hurting

So many people hurting in the world
They just don't know where to go
Just really longing for relief
They don't let friends and family know!

Keeping their pain, to themselves
They wonder what life is for
They feel like just giving up
Not wanting to take anymore!

I've talked to the Lord about this
And told Him that I want to help them out
Just show them hope and love
Because I know what pain is about!

Some people struggle all their life
But don't want to leave their family
They're just thinking about a way out
Because happy they want to be!

I've been down this road many times
And only the Lord has gotten me through
I felt at times like giving up
But, it's not what I really wanted to do!

I know God's making beauty out of my ashes
He has something in store for me
I'm not sure what it is yet
But someday I will see!

Diamonds in the Rough

We never know what people are going through
But sometimes I can see pain on their face
I can see the desperation in their eyes
To get to a better place!

So, I pray to God to help someone
And let me have a listening ear
To show these people love and concern
So in this life , they'll want to be here!

Diamonds in the Rough

Healed By His Touch

You didn't have all bad times
Good things God gave to you
Like feeling the oceans breeze on your face
And surfing the mighty waves too!

I saw you with happiness on your face
Many times overcome with joy
No one could even tell anything was wrong
You just looked like a normal boy!

But I knew what was happening
I could see it most days
Since you were a small child
You were different in your ways!

You didn't know what was going on
So young, three or four
I would get tears in my eyes
Not knowing what life had in store!

We went through the doctors, the crying, the meds
The anxiety and depression too
I just wanted you to be happy all of the time
I wanted a better life for you!

I feel joy when I think about where you are
Even though I miss you so much
I know you're at peace now
You've been healed by the Master's touch!

Diamonds in the Rough

In His Hands

I feel that I am quite strong
Because of things that I've been through
There are many trials and tribulations
The bible says its true!

In my earlier days, sad things happened
But I was able to make it through
And as things are right now
I am going through sad times too!

Life holds many mysteries
That we can't figure out
So many questions we ask
Trying to figure out what life's about!

My help comes from my Father
He's the one that's kept me sane
Whatever I am going through
In this storm, in the downpour of rain!

I've never asked Him, why me?
When tragedies come my way
Because I'm not exempt from pain
And He'll explain it to me someday!

Although my mind and body are struggling
It has to be in God's plan
He gets me through this storm
And He holds me in His hands!

Diamonds in the Rough

The Letter

I know that you're in Heaven, son
And I wish I could send you a letter
It would say I know you're in perfect peace
And I know that you're so much better!

It would say how I've loved you since you were born
And how happy I was to have you
God had truly blessed me
With a special gift that only He knew!

I would tell you how
I adored you
And how I rocked you in my arms all night
How I stayed close to you and didn't let you out of my sight!

It would say you were the apple of my eye
And quite a charming boy
So handsome and compassionate
You brought me so much joy!

And it would say that as you grew older
How I was so proud of you
For giving you time to volunteer
And help save lives too!

I'll never stop loving you, son
Even though you're not here
I know God's taking care of you
Because He whispered in my ear!

Diamonds in the Rough

In Perfect Peace

I saw things getting really worse
But I also saw you push through it
I wondered how far you would go
I don't blame you for leaving one bit!

Although I really am happy that you're at peace
And it's really breaking my heart
But I would never call you back
Even though we have to be apart!

If I could somehow turn back the clock
And had one more chance to help you
Maybe I could have made you listen
But your pain only God knew!

But if you came back and were still in pain
I wouldn't want you to stay
I'd hug you and send you on your way
And know I'd see you someday!

God is getting me through this pain
And I know He's wiped your tears away
I can't wait to see you in perfect peace
I look forward to that day!

Diamonds in the Rough

You're Happy

Now Son, don't ever think you didn't matter
Because you just had to go
I really miss you alot right now
And how I love you so!

I really wish you could've stayed
But you really didn't see a way out
But I knew the Lord could've helped you
I know that without a doubt!

You wouldn't let anyone in
Most of the time you covered your pain
I know how hard it was on you
You probably felt like you were going insane!

I tried to help you the best I could
But you never came to me
I knew you didn't want me to hurt
Sad, you didn't want me to be!

I'm sadder now that you've left
But I'm also happy for you
I know that you're resting with Jesus
And spending time with your dad too!

Diamonds in the Rough

Tired And Weary

My son seemed so weary
So tired and so worn
This life was too much for him
Now I'm left here to morn!

I knew he thought about leaving this world
For a long time, it's true
He was just waiting for the right moment
To do what he had to do!

I saw him so unhappy
I knew things were getting bad
I had a feeling he would leave his life
To go and be with His dad!

I saw it coming years ago
But he really held on for so long
His mental state overtook him
This illness is just so wrong!

Now I'm grieving everyday
So many tears in my eyes
But someday I'll be with him again
And I'll tell this world goodbye!

Diamonds in the Rough

A Special Dream Of You

I awoke with a joyful heart this morning
With tears running down my face
I noticed right away that you were happy in my dream
Because you were in a beautiful place!

In this dream we were together alot
And I enjoyed spending time with you
As I leaned over to kiss you
We both said our goodbyes too!

You told me again, not to be sad
That you had to go away
You said someday Jesus would call me home
And we would reunite on that Glorious day!

It's just that I miss you so much now, son
And you will never have any idea
How much I really love you
And to me, you are so dear!

I realize you had a reason for leaving
And I watched you suffer for years
My mind can understand that
But it's left my heart in tears!

The Lord will help me carry on
This pain He'll get me through
And you'll always be in my heart
Until one day when I see you!

Diamonds in the Rough

All That I Am

My life has changed in the last year
So much that I'll never be the same
This grief isn't going anywhere
Until the Lord someday calls my name!

What an exciting time that will be
When my tears are wiped away
I'll be given a Glorious body
I can't wait until that wonderful day!

I'll ask the Lord why He allowed me to suffer so much
But, maybe it won't matter anymore
This life can't be compared to Heaven
They'll be no pain like we had before!

It's hard to imagine a perfect place
Where we'll get a gold crown and a reward
It seems to good to be true
That forever we'll praise the Lord!

God has given me many blessings in my life
I don't know why He's so good to me
When I cry out to Him, He comes
And all of my tears, He sees!

Lately God has seen my sufferings
And He's promised to bring me through
All that I am, He created
And I know that His love is true!

Diamonds in the Rough

His Pain Will Cease

If we were to come into the Lord's presence
As we are, we'd fall down on our knees
We couldn't comprehend His power
But His holiness , we would see!

We'll receive our Heavenly bodies
And right then we'll understand
All the mysteries of this life
And before the Lord we'll stand!

God will explain so much to us
Like why our loved ones had to be apart
He has all the answers for us
He now sees the humbleness in our hearts!

When I get there, I'll have questions
Ones I've never asked before
But when I see the Lord, I'll know
That my son's not in pain anymore!

I won't be heartbroken when I see him
Because God has given my son, peace
And I'll finally understand then
That he left so his suffering would cease!

Diamonds in the Rough

The Best Son Of All

The Best Son Of All
When you were just a baby
You were my pride and joy
I thanked God for you A sweet and precious baby boy!

I spoiled you every chance I got
But your dad didn't like that one bit
I'd sing to you for hours
In the old rocking chair we'd sit!

I just couldn't believe that you were mine
I had prayed for you a few years
The Lord certainly blessed us
When I first held you, I broke into big tears!

The years went by and you grew so fast
Where had my little boy gone?
I knew even though you didn't need me as much
We'd always still have that bond!

Nothing could ever get in the way
Of my unfailing love for you
The moment that I first held you
I knew that love was true!

Even though you're gone now
My love for you still stands tall
I'm so privilege to have been your mother
You were the best son of all!

Diamonds in the Rough

You'll Know Him

I remember the day that you left
I didn't know it would be the end
I hugged you tight, and said goodbye
The Lord knew where you had been!

You would pretend and not show your feelings
But I knew something wasn't right
I saw the sadness in your eyes
And it seemed to get worse at night!

You would come up to visit me
And I asked if there was anything I could do
But you said that you were ok
I said I love and miss you too!

I knew that you put up a fight
For many years, everyday
It really broke my heart to know
That there was nothing I could do or say!

I saw you go down a long, hard road
You must have thought you were going insane
It didn't seem to be any sunshine in your life
Just a stormy downpour of rain!

Although you leaving has broken my heart
But I don't have to worry anymore
I truly know you're with the Lord
And you'll know Him like never before!

Diamonds in the Rough

Where The Skies Are Blue

I'm thinking about what you're doing, son
Since you got your wings
Are you just roaming around through Heaven?
Enjoying the peace God brings?

When you entered through the gates of pearl
I know there was a smile upon your face
When you laid your eyes on Jesus
And all your pain He erased!

You use to be excited about Heaven
What I taught you when you were a boy
You ask me lots of questions
Your voice was just full of joy!

You asked me what forever meant
Are there Angels really there?
And do they fly around with their wings?
And sing praises everywhere?

You really listened to me as I talked to you
And you then believed that my words were true
I told you someday you'd be going there
To Heaven, with the skys painted blue!

I just know you're there with Jesus
And you have so much to say
You're just waiting for Him to bring me home
I can't wait until that day!

Diamonds in the Rough

He Makes Me Stronger

I walk down to my garden each day
And I glance over at your tree
The one I planted in memory of you
So sad it is to me!

Although I sit there for a moment
And I wonder what you're doing up there
I really feel that you're happy
With no more pain to bear!

God knew what He was doing
When He called you home that night
I knew you were longing for Heaven
Oh, what a beautiful sight!

No suffering and heartache there
And that makes me happy as I can be
Knowing that one day we'll be together
God's brought you a peace that I will see!

I know that I will grieve for you
For a long time I feel
But God will be right beside me
In order that I may heal!

He's been the one that's gotten me through
When I didn't think I could go any longer
He gives me a peace that passes all understanding
He comes to me and I'm stronger!

Diamonds in the Rough

I'll See You, Again

I'm thinking about how much of your life that you've missed
As I thumb through pictures of you
I've been feeling really sad these days
Because my heart's just crushed into!

I'm aware that a year has gone by
And it seems that I'm grieving even more
I just really miss you so much
Longing for you to walk right through that door!

I know you'd been thinking about your misery a long time
And you were looking for a way to get out
I just wish you had come to me
And talked about these feelings that you felt!

I know you were sad alot in this life
And it made me feel sad for you
Only the Lord knew the extent of your suffering
He knew how you were feeling inside too!

I know where you are is so much better
There's no more pain and heartache for you
I would never call you back for a moment
To give you what you went through!

I really love you so much, my son
And I'm relieved that I'll see you again
But for now the Lord is getting me through
I can always depend on Him!

Diamonds in the Rough

God Has Been Good To Me

The Lord has really been good to me
Although I'm heartbroken inside
It doesn't change His love for me
Because in me, He does abide!

A year ago when my son passed
I might not have seen it this way
Although I wasn't angry, I still wondered
Why he had to go away !

I already know the answer
But it doesn't erase the pain inside
Such a tragic way it happened
I've been grieving since the day he died!

The pain and suffering won't go away
Just because I want it to
It will stay with me for years
Because of the deep love I had for you!

There's no doubt that God will get me through
I depend on Him so much
And I know He's got you in His hands
Healed by a simple touch!

I owe the Lord, for everything I am
He has made me that way
And I'm using it for His glory
I can't wait to see Him someday!

Diamonds in the Rough

His Pain And Heartache Are Done

I use to worry about my children
And the anxiety caused me pain
Sometimes deep depression set in
I often felt like I was going insane!

I talked to the Lord today
And I told Him the anxiety I had, came true
I never thought my child would go before me
But, all along, God knew!

He knew my son, inside and out
And knew the sufferings he had
Little did I know he'd be leaving
To go reunite with his dad!

I know why the Lord allowed it to happen
Even though it was a tragedy
He knew what my sons future would be like
A long, sad life He could see!

So God answered my prayer that I prayed
To heal my sons mind, if He would
No one else had done that
The Lord was the only one that could!

So He answered my prayer that night
And He brought peace to my son
I know now why God allowed this
To make the pain and heartache, be done!

Diamonds in the Rough

Words God's Given Me

I haven't questioned the purpose of being here
After my son had passed away
I still have family here for me
And I know that God will get me through each day!

I know He sees my sufferings
And what it's done to me
But He also knows that I trust Him
And someday the reasons, I'll see!

It feels good using my poetry to help others
When some can't get their words out
The words that express their feelings
Of what their pain and heartache are about!

The Lord gave me this gift years ago
He tells me every word to write
He's longing for everyone to lean on Him
And turn their darkness into light!

God knows how much our pain is
And He helps us to get through
And I know if I could've depend on Him
I don't know what I would do!

I just trust that God knows all things
He's proven that to me
He's been here in my darkest moments
Because peace He wants to bring me!

Diamonds in the Rough

Through Each Day

Above the Heavenly skies I know
That there's a home just waiting for me
I might not get there for awhile
But someday with my Lord, I'll be!

The pain and suffering down here will be gone
And He'll wipe my tears away
Then I'll be reunited with my son
I look forward to that wonderful day!

Many things in my life I don't understand
But someday God will let it be known
There was a reason at times, I didn't trust Him
And why I felt so all alone!

The Lord looked down and saw my son's pain
And knew he couldn't make it any longer
He knew that his leaving would be hard on me
But He knew that He'd make me stronger!

I don't blame God for my pain and heartache
And for a life that could've been
The Lord knew about my son's suffering
And He knew him before the world began!

I do trust in the Lord for everything
No matter what comes my way
I know that He'll never leave me
And He'll get me through each day!

Diamonds in the Rough

I'll Rise Above The Pain

I'm keeping your Facebook page open
So I can scroll through pictures of you
And when I see one of you smiling
It makes me feel happy too!

In a lot of your pictures you're looking so sad
And I wonder what was going on
All the bad days outweighed the good
And that makes my heart feel torn!

I didn't know for sure why this happened
And I didn't know how your heart made you feel
But I do know that I prayed to God
That your mind would one day be healed!

I guess that's the reason God took you home
Because He couldn't answer my prayer in that way
He had other plans for you
He decided to let you come home, that day! Eve

n though we can't understand why this happens
Why the good can't outweigh the bad
We'll just have to accept these things in life
And it still makes me feel so sad!

I have many memories of you
They're in my heart to stay
And someday I will see you again
I can't wait until that day!

Diamonds in the Rough

For now I'll try to rise above the pain
Although it's the hardest thing I've done
To not have you here with me
I love and miss you so much, my son!

Diamonds in the Rough

My Dream Of You

I thought I saw you the other day
Or maybe it was in my dreams
You were looking around for me
And peace was given to you, it seemed!

Yes, you were so happy that day
Like I'd never seen you before
God had answered you prayer finally
And the pain you'd had was no more!

It made me feel so wonderful
To see you with a carefree heart
To feel like you've never felt before
Because of the peace God brought!

Someday the Lord will do the same for me
And you and I will be together
Just loving our Heavenly Father
And it will be that way forever!

So, for now I'll just move ahead
And make it the best I can
I know there's nothing that I should fear
Because God's got me in His hands!

Diamonds in the Rough

My Heart May Heal

I'm hurting more for you now, son
It just doesn't seem that real
The way it happened, the way you left
I know that you tried, but couldn't heal!

What could I have done differently?
The question is on my mind
Maybe I couldn't have done anything
Because peace you just wanted to find!

It was your time, you'd had enough
It was nothing I could have done to stop you
My aching heart is just full of pain
I just love and miss you too!

I know the answers to my questions
But, still I ask myself why?
Why couldn't you have a normal life?
Now I just sit and cry!

I know this grief will slow down someday
And maybe this pain inside will be gone
But this grief has taken over me
Because we had a tight bond!

So, I'll try to hold my head up high
And just try to get through each day
I've never stopped loving you
Since the time that you went away!

Diamonds in the Rough

Fill Me With Your Peace

Come fill me with your peace, Lord
And make me whole again
This hard road that I'm traveling
Only You know where I have been!

Many times during my life
I've wondered if I could make it through
I didn't feel close to the Lord
So, I didn't know what to do!

Time moved on and I was a wreck
Having to suffer all alone
I questioned sometimes if you even cared
All the pain in my life, you've known!

I finally hit rock bottom
And my heart was crying out
I sought you one lonely night
I needed to know what your love was all about!

You gave me love like I'd never known
And you wiped my tears away
You never left me for a moment
And you're still with me, today!

I regret not finding you sooner
I don't know why I waited so long
My life didn't feel worth living
It just felt terribly wrong!

Diamonds in the Rough

I'm so happy you're in my life
To help me through the pain and tears
I just know you'll never leave me
In my heart I hold you dear!

Diamonds in the Rough

God Gives Me Strength

Your birthday was on a Saturday last year
And the same morning I was told
That you had passed, knowing you weren't coming back
It hurt far down into my soul!

It still hurts there and I am scared
That this pain won't go away
Although I've been told it will
It seems like it's here to stay!

I know in my heart that God won't leave me
But He knows this grief is going to take while
I know He has been here all along
While I'm going through this trial!

I guess He knows that I am strong
To allow this to happen to me
I know God has plans for my future
But, right now I just can't see!

I sometimes worry about my family here
 That something will happen to them too
I hear that this is quite normal
Because of the tragedy I've been through!

I won't move on by myself
Because the Lord wouldn't want me to
He wants me to fully trust Him
And that's what I'm going to do!

Diamonds in the Rough

I know for sure I'll see my son again
I don't know how long it will be
But, when my life is finished here
There will be a home in Heaven for me!

Diamonds in the Rough

You're On My Mind

I'm just sitting here with you on my mind
Knowing that I'll get along
It's so hard to grasp what happened
But I know that I am strong!

The Lord gets me through this time
But there's still pain in my heart
It's just that it's part of grieving
Because my son and I are apart!

It gave me a broken heart when you left
And my heart is still broken today
I didn't know when you left last time
That you'd be going away!

I want to watch videos of you
When you were just a boy
I loved you being my son
You brought me a much joy!

But I know if I watch them
Tears will be running down my face
But, then I'll have to remind myself
That you're in a better place!

I'm sorry you had to leave so soon
And I truly understand
That you wanted to be at peace
And have God hold you in His hands!

Diamonds in the Rough

You're Healed By The Master's Touch

A year has gone by so fast
And I'm still brokenhearted some days
I know I'm strong enough to get through this
Many days I go to God and pray!

It's just the waves of grief hit me
And most times it takes my breath
But I really just count on God
While I am grieving your death!

I know in the back of my mind sometimes
I had a feeling you would go this way
I realized you needed to leave
But I really wanted you to stay!

I saw your illness get ahold of you
And most times it wouldn't let go
You kept it from me for so long
You always seemed so low!

All that's left now is memories
I go through your photo book
Tears just run down my face
Because of your life you took!

I'll never forget you, my son
You'll be on my mind so much
And I'll never forget your home in Heaven
And how you've been healed by your Master's touch!

Diamonds in the Rough

My Precious Boy

I got the devastating news that morning
That my only son had passed on
My precious boy, I loved him
Since the day that he was born!

It's broken my heart to lose him
And to know that he left by his own hand
He was a special, compassionate person
He'd turned into a fine young man!

I knew something was wrong for a while
But he never opened up to me
I went to him wanting to help
Peaceful I wanted him to be!

I didn't know how much he was suffering
It is such a shame
Sometimes I feel guilty
Thinking maybe I'm to blame!

I should have pushed him harder
And made him listen to me
But most of the time, he was stubborn
And left alone, he wanted to be!

I knew his depression had gotten worse
But I just didn't know what to do
I watched him as he went downhill
And he finally gave up, I knew!

Diamonds in the Rough

I know now that my son is at peace
God's got him in His hands
And one day the Lord will explain to me
What in this life I didn't understand!

Diamonds in the Rough

Mesmerized

I had another dream about you
And you took me to your home
The home that I recognized to be Heaven
A place where you never have to be alone!

I was so mesmerized by its beauty
More beautiful than I thought it would be
Mountains, rivers and lakes
So many sights to see!

And I heard the Angels voices
It was like nothing I'd heard before
A sound that just took my breath away
I wanted to hear much more!

But then it was time to meet
Jesus My Savior, the King of Kings
I've waited for so long
To have the perfect peace that He brings!

I've never felt this way before
I just can't believe we're here
I know I will have to leave soon
But I long for Him to wipe away my tears!

I am so happy for you now
It is the best dream I've ever had
And I know that one day I'll be there
Together with you and your dad!

Diamonds in the Rough

Can't Wait To See You

I can't wait to see my son with wings
Just flying through the air
Wearing a pristine robe so white
And without a worry or care!

Yes, this day will be so special It's a day
I've been waiting for
Looking forward to seeing my family
Pain and tears will be no more!

I'll just thank the Lord for bringing me home
To a mansion He's prepared for me
Heaven will be so Glorious
A real Paradise to see!

I haven't done anything to deserve this
But God loves me anyway
He sent His Son two thousand years ago
To prepare me for this day!

Just in an instant I'm there with Jesus
Just the One I've been longing to meet
I'll be mesmerized by His beauty
And I'll fall down at His feet!

Don't worry now son, I could see you soon
You just don't know from day to day
When that day is coming
The day He wipes my tears away!

Diamonds in the Rough

Grieving You

I'm feeling kinda sad today
Just thinking that you're not here
I'm tired of grieving so much
And I'm tired of shedding tears!

It's not getting any better
I thought the pain would be gone by now
Wish I could make it leave
But I don't really know how!

So, I just put on my grieving gear
And get ready to tackle another day
I call out to the Lord
Please take this misery away!

He gives me the strength to carry on
I'm still so tired of this grief
It haunts me night and day
God please bring me some relief!

Relief will come for a little while
Then the waves hit once more
They're really knocking me under
I feel like I'm fighting a war!

But God really gives me His strength
If He didn't, it would be pretty bad
It's just that I'm missing you so much
And thinking about the memories I have!

Diamonds in the Rough

I know someday I'll see you once more
I just pray God gets me through
Through the pain and tears
That I cry for you!

Diamonds in the Rough

He Has Me In His Hands

I know life is unfair at times
With so much suffering and pain
Sometimes you're at the end of your rope
You feel as if you're going insane!

I've gotten to that point many times in my life
I felt like I couldn't go on
What was the purpose of me living
Why was I even born?

There were many years that I didn't have God
I had to get through struggles on my own
But all along He was there
Although I felt so all alone!

Why was He even allowing this
Much pain and anxiety too
Sometimes I questioned God
My sufferings He already knew!

He knew that I couldn't understand His plan
It was too hard to figure it out
I couldn't call on the Lord when I should've
I had no clue what it was all about!

He caught up with me years later
And I asked Him to rescue me
He came and put His arms around me
Peaceful God wanted me to be!

Diamonds in the Rough

So now I trust Him completely
I never doubt His plan
Because I know when I need Him
God holds me in His hands!

Diamonds in the Rough

Peaceful I Will Be

Please someone tell me now
That this pain will one day be gone
I'm really struggling so hard
But I know that I am strong!

God gives me strength that I need
To get through this tragedy
He takes me to a better place
And peace He brings to me!

Most people don't know, not a clue
At the pain we Mothers are in
We really try to grieve softer
So our hearts maybe will mend!

Sometimes the pain is unbearable
But I try my best to get through
I love and miss you, my son
And this grief is for you!

I have no doubt where you are
I feel better knowing you're pain free
And someday I will join you
And peaceful I will be!

Diamonds in the Rough

Nothing Has Prepared Me

I've seen clouds and sunshine
And I've seen fire and rain
But nothing has prepared me
For this terrible pain!

It's a pain like I've never felt
It just reaches down into my soul
It's because I'm missing my son
Him, I just want to hold!

Time is passing pretty fast
It's already been a year
A year since my heart was broken
My boy, I hold so dear!

I guess some think I should move on
But, they don't have a clue
To lose a child in a tragic way
Is really hard to get through

I'm fighting these feelings the best I can
And the waves that come
It's really been hard on me
I wish the pain would ease up some!

Son, you'll always be in my heart
I have so many memories of you
I have to continue on this journey
Just know I love and miss you too!

Diamonds in the Rough

Memories Of You

We spent a week at the beach every Summer
And we all had a lot of fun
I'll never forget our time together
I'm really missing you, my son!

I watched you as you reeled in a big fish
Off of the pier that day
You were so proud of yourself
You wanted this moment to stay!

At the beach you rode your boogie board
You were studying each wave
Waiting for the perfect one
You were feeling so brave!

I enjoyed walking the beach with you at night
Listening to the sound the waves made
Feeling so peaceful and carefree
If only these feelings could have stayed!

When it was time to pack up for home
I know it made you feel sad
You liked spending time with your family
Remembering the fun days we had!

These memories I keep in my heart
Are going to be here to stay
And someday we'll be together again
I can't wait for that Glorious day!

Diamonds in the Rough

I'll Never Give Up

I promised God that I'd never give up
No matter what might come my way
I think I've been through the worst part
Someday I might be ok!

But for now, I must travel on
And this road gets really rough
But God tells me of His promise
He knows when I've had enough!

All of my life I've fought this fight
Never knowing what the outcome would be
The Lord has looked down from above
A better life He wants for me!

I think I may be struggling the hardest now
Pain like I've never had before
My heart's just torn in two
I ask God not to give me anymore!

My eyes are filled with tears these days
Because I'm missing you, son
The images fill my mind
And I'm thinking about what you've done!

I will never blame you for leaving this way
I knew the pain you were in
So you prayed and told the Lord
That you were ready for it to end!

Diamonds in the Rough

It's broken my heart to lose you
And I know I'll see you someday
But my heart has been longing for you
Since the day you passed away!

Diamonds in the Rough

God Can Bring Us Peace

Sometimes the days are full of rain
And other days, the sun shines so bright
So many times I've talked to you
Even though you're nowhere in sight!

I realize you're not going to answer me
But somehow it just eases my mind
And I pray for God to help me
Someday maybe happiness I'll find!

I looked forward to you having a family
Maybe it would have helped you cope
I really didn't know how to comfort you
I just wanted you to have some hope!

I prayed that God would heal you
Like He did for me a few years ago
His healing would be the answer
And peace and joy, you'd know!

The Lord's ways are not ours
He has plans that we don't see
He wraps His arms around us
Peaceful He wants us to be!

I'm feeling that peace a little bit
But I have a long way to go
The Lord is bringing me through this
And I'm here son, loving you so!

Diamonds in the Rough

I'll See You Again

There are many days that I am sad
But at times I have good days too
I wonder how long this will last
This pain from missing you!

I've never had pain like this before
Even though I've lost close loved ones
My heart is just crushed in two
Because I'm grieving for you, son!

Oh, it hurts sometimes so bad
I can't do this much longer
I pray to God to help me
And He comes and makes me stronger!

No one told me it would hurt this much
While I'm loving and missing you
It's a love that lasted your lifetime
And I'm having a time grieving too!

I'll move on someday when I'm ready
I don't want to rush this through
It could take a while for me to heal
I don't want others to rush me too!

I feel one day the worse pain will be softer
And maybe my heart will mend
But for now I'll continue loving you
And can't wait to see you again!

Diamonds in the Rough

Since The Day You Were Born

The days and months have gone by so fast
It's been over a year
I thought that my grieving would lessen
I just really need you here!

Not for long, just a little while
I just wanted to tell you how I feel
If I could just talk to you
I think my heart would start to heal!

I want to tell you what you meant to me
And how I loved you so much
When you were here in this world
And now you're healed by the Lords touch!

When you were born, how I adored you
I showered you with love
And someone else looking down on you
It was the Lord from above!

You grew so fast , I couldn't believe it
That you'd grown up to be a fine young man
I dedicated you to God And
He had you in His hands!

Now your life down here has vanished
But I know where you are
Sometimes you come to me
And it doesn't make Heaven seem to far!

Diamonds in the Rough

So I'm excited that I'll see you again
But now I have to go on
But just remember that I love you
Since the day that you were born!

Diamonds in the Rough

A Place For Us In Heaven

I'm looking at my bird feeder in the window
Hoping a cardinal will stop by
They always remind me of you
When I see one, I just cry!

I haven't seen any signs from you lately
And I know that you're just fine
You're so at peace and happy
But, I still can't get you off my mind!

I'll be down by your tree a lot
Because my garden is there
I'll just sit and talk to you
Sometimes this pain is hard to bear!

It seems like you just left here
But, it's already been a year
Where does the time go?
I just want to feel you near!

I have things on my mind about you
I'm just thinking back to that night
I have painful images of you
That you gave it your last fight!

I love you so much, my son
And I know that I'll see you again someday
You'll tell me a lot about your new home
The place where we will stay!

Diamonds in the Rough

The Lord Blesses Me

In my life God has blessed me tremendously
Even when I couldn't see
And He's always been here
He's really been good to me!

I call on the Lord when I'm hurting
And He's right here by my side
At times this struggle is so hard
With all my might, I've tried!

When tragedies come my way
And I can barely stand I know
I can't do this alone
So I know He holds me in His hands!

God has seen every tear that I have cried
And He knows I struggle every day
He wants to bring me peace
And wipe these tears away!

Sometimes I can't feel Him here
The times that it gets pretty rough
I still go to Him in prayer
And tell Him I've had enough!

He knows what I can handle
He won't put too much on me
And He sees my heart is broken
Much pain He knows it will be!

Diamonds in the Rough

He longs to bring my heart peace
So I can be on my way
To get through this suffering
That I fight so hard everyday!

Diamonds in the Rough

Mental Illness Is Horror

A mental illness can be awful
You can live with much horror
Somedays you don't think you can't make it
You think you'll be dead by tomorrow!

You can see and hear things that aren't there
It's especially scary at night
You try to just ride it out
You're fighting it with all your might!

It can last a lifetime
It can be there every single day
You're dealing with it the best you can
But it will not go away!

I've lived with this for years and years
It's just a life of misery
You keep it hidden inside your mind
So that no one will see!

It really doesn't surprise me
When I hear of a suicide
They die by their own hands
They tried to hide their pain inside!

Finally, a few years ago
With Gods help, He healed my mind
I had prayed for that a long time
Because this illness was never kind!

Diamonds in the Rough

So now I'm free from the depression
That could torture me everyday
I'm just thankful to the Lord
For finally taking it away!

Diamonds in the Rough

He's Been There For Me

The Lord wants to help you out
So please don't turn the other way
He has so many blessings for you
It will change your night and day!

He has truly been so good to me
Even though I didn't deserve it
He comes when I call out to Him
He come to me and sits!

He has given me His mercy and grace
He has really been a friend to me
A friend like no other
Grateful I will always be!

God sees the tears that I cry
These tears are not in vain
He knows my every move
And He knows my pain!

His promises to us are true
He does what He says He'll do
He has your best interest at heart
And He really does love you!

I turned to Him, years ago
It was the best thing I've ever done
He promised to get me through
God wanted me to have His only Son!

Diamonds in the Rough

So, now I call on Him so much
And He never gets tired of me
He's given me love like I've never known
Peaceful He wants me to be!

Diamonds in the Rough

God Sees Our Pain

This world can be so full of pain
Many sufferings and much tragedy
It affects some more than others
God looks down and sees!

He sees people trying to get through by themselves
Never giving Him any thought
He longs for us to call on Him
And He loves us with all His heart!

I've been through so much pain in my life
At times I've left God out
But now I rely on Him
He gets me through without a doubt!

I don't know what I'd do without Him
I cry and He hears my plea
I go to Him so brokenhearted
And He comes to rescue me!

It would help so many people
If the Lord, they'd turn to
He sees every tear you cry
And wants to be your Savior too!

He has proven to me His love
He gives me His mercy and grace
And when I call out to Him
He comes to me without haste!

Diamonds in the Rough

God's Getting Me Through

Many months have gone by now
And I haven't seen your face
I know someday that I will
But, now you're in a better place!

At times I've cried myself to sleep
With you on my mind
It's hard to believe you've gone
And you've left me behind!

I knew the condition of your mind and heart
You were living in pain for many years
I noticed the sadness in your eyes
That released of lot of tears!

God has explained to me over time
That your illness wasn't going away
He truly saw your sufferings
During that tragedy, He was there that day!

You're absent has broken my heart and soul
And I'm really trying to hang on
I know you're in Heaven so peaceful
I've loved you since the day you were born!

So the Lord is helping me through this
He knows what I'm going through
And He has promised to wipe away my tears
And reunite with you one day!

Diamonds in the Rough

We Know They're At Peace

I put my new birdbath in my garden
Beside the tree I planted for you
I go there often to visit
Talking to you is what I like to do!

I miss you so incredibly much
Since the day that you've been gone
Since you were a little boy
We always had that bond!

A bond between a mother and son
Is a bond that never goes away
That bond is built on love
And it's in my heart to stay!

So, I sit there by your tree
Tears running down my face
And even though I'm feeling so sad
I realize you in a wonderful place!

No, I couldn't call you back
To go through that pain you were in
I know you're now resting peacefully
You'll never have to go through it again!

I try to see the good that's happened
God's turning my ashes into beauty
It's my desire to help others
And it's exactly where I want to be!

Diamonds in the Rough

My poems that I write are helping people
And it really feels good to me
I know what they're going through
Their pain and heartache I see!

We're all in this together
And we're going to come out ok
We know our children are happy
And we know we'll see them one day!

Diamonds in the Rough

I'm Busy Missing You

I got the news that you were missing
Your girlfriend called me that night
She said you just left so fast
You were gone, out of sight!

The officers searched for you there
You left with only your gun and your phone
I tried to call you with no luck
I feel you were so alone!

A neighbor saw you pacing back and forth
If I could have just got to you
I know you felt anguish in your mind
You had a severe illness too!

That Saturday morning, I got a knock on the door
It was a detective there to give me the news
He said that you had taken your life
He was there to tell me the truth!

It was your birthday that day
Which really made it worse
I just broke down right away
I felt like my heart would burst!

I just sat and stared out the window
I was in shock they told me
There were a lot of people in the room
They came to be with me!

Diamonds in the Rough

That's been a year ago
And my heart is still crushed in two
I'm trying my best to get through
But I've been busy missing you!

Diamonds in the Rough

God's Presence

I walked to my garden early this morning
And I felt Gods presence there,
I asked Him to come and help me
Because this pain is hard to bear!

I think I heard Him speak to me
And tell me He will always be here
I know that He loves me
And always holds me dear!

He told me it would take a while
For this grief to end
To give it to Him completely
Because He knows where I've been!

I listened to Him , and started to pray
Tears rolling down my face
I told Him that I wish my son were here
He told me that he was in a better place!

I know he's in perfect peace
His pain has been washed away
The Lord is taking care of him
And I'll see him again someday!

I know the grief may someday fade
And my eyes will dry up too
But for now I will push through this
While I'm longing for you!!!

Diamonds in the Rough

This Crippling Disease

This horrible disease is crippling our Nation
This mental illness that's here
I've delt with it for my whole life
It's taking our children that we hold dear!

The pain they're in is hard to describe
And it can get pretty bad
Now my son is gone and missed
A life he could have had!

I feel he could have gotten better
Giving the right help and meds
But he wouldn't try to help himself
I just couldn't get inside his head!

These young people don't realize how important they are
That God loves them so much
And if they could give Him their pain
They could be healed by the Master's touch!

God has been here for me
When my depression got pretty tough
I would feel like giving up
I felt I'd had enough!

People are feeling ashamed to talk about their illness
A weakness some think it could be
But this is not what is happening
Only a few people can see!

Diamonds in the Rough

I know my son is in peace now
Happier than he ever dreamed he could be
There with his loving Father
And that's good enough for me!

Diamonds in the Rough

If You Could Come Back

If you could just come back and live your life
Then I would trade places with you
If you could live in peace and happiness
And not live the life that you knew!

Your life would be so different
To live your days with joy
I'd be so happy for you
You are my son, my precious boy!

To see you actually enjoying your life
No pain or heartache for you
Making plans for your future
And maybe starting a family too!

All these things, you've missed
And that makes me so sad
To leave this world so suddenly
A life that you could've had!

I know this life wasn't for you
Because of the illness in your mind
I just wanted you to live your life
But, peace and happiness, you couldn't find!

I know that the life that you're living now
Can never compare to life here
The Lord has truly set you free
And wiped away your tears!

Diamonds in the Rough

The Lord Can Get Them Through

So many people taking their lives
They're just tired of this fight
They've wrestled it as long as they could
They've fought it with all their might!

No one knows the extent of their suffering
And the times they feel like they're going insane
Most people don't have a clue
Of their sadness and pain!

I've traveled down this winding road
It's on a road you don't want to be
Just dead ends and sorrow
It was a place that terrified me!

I know how much pain my son was in
He didn't have to say a word
I could just look into his eyes
And crying sometimes I heard!

He fought so hard like everyone else
But he got tired after a while
I could see how sad he was
I barely ever saw him smile!

We need to reach these people
Show them that there's a way out
Tell them of God's love for them
How He can help them, without a doubt!

Diamonds in the Rough

I'd Hold You Tight

If I could just hold you tight
I'd never let you go
To wrap my arms around you
My love for you would show!

You'll never know how much I love you
And the way I miss you so much
But I think you're at peace now
You're healed by the Master's touch!

If I could just see your face
And see you smiling at me
It would make me feel so peaceful
To see you there, pain free!

If I could walk through Heaven with you
And see all the sights
There's no darkness there
Just Gods light shinning bright!

I'd want to meet Jesus first
The Savoir that saved my soul
I would see his nail scarred hands
His body I'd want to hold!

I know I would feel whole again
The Lord would wipe my tears away
The pain in me would just vanish
I can't wait for that Glorious day!

Diamonds in the Rough

Poems For You

I've written many poems about my son
Don't know what else to write about
He's the one that's in my heart
This, I have no doubt!

I think that writing about him
Maybe helps me feel better
I just can't wait to see him again
I'll be there with him forever!

I long to be in Heaven
Because you are there
And your dad is there beside you
No worries and no cares!

Your dad went years before you
And I know it broke your heart
But now your reunited
And you'll never be apart!

I know you're happy and at peace
I couldn't ask for anything better for you
Just being there with Jesus
And doing what you were meant to do!

I look so forward to seeing you again
I can't wait to be in my Heavenly home
To be with all of my family
And throughout Heaven, we'll roam!

Diamonds in the Rough

What A Glorious Day

You're really on my mind today
I cry these tears for you
I don't know how long it will take
I'm doing the best I can do!

I think back to the day I saw you
That image is always in my mind
You looked like you were sleeping
Peace you just wanted to find!

I wanted to touch your arm
And your hand I just wanted to hold
When I leaned over to kiss you goodbye
Your face felt so cold!

I couldn't believe it was really you
I'd just seen you two days before
I told you goodbye and I love you
As you were walking out that door!

I know you fought the best you could
I saw you struggle through the years
I would have done anything for you
It really brought me to tears!

I know that you're at peace now, son
And God's wiped your tears away
I look forward to seeing you again
Oh, what a Glorious Day!

Diamonds in the Rough

If I Could Visit Heaven

If I could see you as you are
And visit Heaven one day
I think that I would know
That I would want to stay!

To be there with you through Eternity
And to feel the peace God brings
To find my family that are there
And hearing the Angels sing!

I wouldn't want to come back
Not to this painful Earth
I'd know the peace God brings
And I would know my worth!

If you could just meet me at the gate
The one made of pearl
And walk me through out Heaven
And introduce me to God's world!

All my pain would be taken away
And God would wipe away my tears
Just mesmerized by the beauty
And beautiful music I'd hear!

I know that I can't leave right now
Because what would my family do?
But don't you worry about me, son
Because one day I'll be with you!

Diamonds in the Rough

I'd Rather Have You In Heaven

I'd rather have you in Heaven
Then suffering here, so bad
My mind is on you all the time
Thinking about the pain you had!

You were just a little boy
When this illness started with you
I felt so sad inside
Because I couldn't help you!

It was so hard, I know
It just broke my heart in two
To watch you live in sadness
I didn't know what to do!

When you reached your teen years
Things just started falling apart
With anxiety and depression
Pain and suffering it brought!

Screaming rages, all the time
Saying you wanted to die
That you hated your life
Getting through it, I know you tried!

But it wasn't hard enough
To ward off the monster inside
You tried to keep it from me
You feelings you wanted to hide!

Diamonds in the Rough

I know I have to get through this grief
But, then I think of you
And how you're at peace now
All of your sufferings, God knew!

So, I'll try harder to deal with this
Because I know that you're pain free
And I have no doubt that I'll see you again
So joyful I will be!

Diamonds in the Rough

These Waves Of Grief

At times, I feel I'm being rushed to grieve
Just to get it out of the way
It's easier said, than done
So I will continue to grieve everyday!

Grief is strange to me sometimes
The waves of pain just hit me
They come unexpected
Tear-filled eyes people will see!

Some things remind me of my son
When I'm out somewhere
That's when the wave hits
And I'm left standing there!

Tears running down my face
Trying to hide it well
I am just so overcome
Those around can tell!

How long will this grief last?
I wish it would give me a break
I'm fighting it the best I can
Don't know how much more I can take!

I think I've made some progress
But there's a ways to go
But with Gods strength, I'll make it
This I surely know!

Diamonds in the Rough

My Memories Of Us

I want to take a walk down memory lane
There are so many memories there
So many that I have of you
In my mind they're everywhere!

I was so happy when I heard,
That I was having a son
A boy just like his dad
Together they'll have fun!

When I brought you home that day
I just held you in my arms
I told myself I would protect you
To keep you from any harm!

You really brought me so much joy
I thanked God for blessing me
For giving me a precious son
A great boy you would be!

Before I had your sister
I spent lots of time with you
We'd go on adventures here
A lot of fun things to do!

Then time quickly moved along
And you weren't that same boy
Sadness and anxiety set in
You didn't have happiness or joy!

Diamonds in the Rough

It's broken my heart to lose you
I hold those memories in my heart
And one day, I'll be with you
And we'll never have to be apart!

Diamonds in the Rough

I Love You To The Moon

No one loved you like I did
And no one knew your pain
So much sadness in your heart
You walked through each downpour of rain!

If I could have just found a way
To bring your heart some joy
I tried but, it wasn't enough
You were my son, my only boy!

I knew what you went through
Because I've been down that road
Sometimes it comes to a dead end
And you're carrying a heavy load!

I hate this illness that took you from me
I knew you'd had enough
Through the pain and suffering
It got pretty rough!

I just wanted to take your pain
I'd asked God to give it to me
So you could have a good life
So peaceful you would be!

I love you to the moon and back
And although this has been so hard on me
I know that you're in perfect peace
And someday I will see!

Diamonds in the Rough

God's Bottling Up My Tears

I thought I was doing alright yesterday
But then a wave of grief hits me
My eyes well up with tears
The purpose of this. I can't see!

I know it's going to take much time
For my broken heart to grieve
And I know who'll help me through this
It's the Lord, I do believe!

He has gotten me this far
And He'll take me the rest of the way
I just have to trust Him with this
I know He'll always stay!

He sees so many tears that I cry
And He's bottling up each one
And He sees the pain inside me
That's there because I've lost my son!

It's the worse pain that I've ever felt
It sometimes just takes my breath away
I just use God's strength and my own
To make it through each day!

I know you're resting peacefully
And I won't be there for a while
But, when I do, I'll be so thrilled
To see you again, my child!

Diamonds in the Rough

God's Taken Your Pain Away

When you were a little boy
You always aimed to please me
Bringing me flowers from my garden
So happy I would be!

You were differently a mama's boy
From the very start
I just couldn't believe you were mine
So much joy you brought!

As you got older, I knew something was wrong
When your smile turned into tears
I just often saw you unhappy
As you went through the years!

The meds they gave you helped a little
But I still saw the pain in your face
Not knowing how to deal with it
I just wanted you to get to a better place!

As you aged it seemed to get worse
I didn't know what to do for you
We would have our rounds each day
You were suffering, that I knew!

I'm so sorry that you had to live this way
I wish there were something I could've done
I tried so hard to help you through this
You were my boy, my only son!

Diamonds in the Rough

I know right now, you're at peace
God's taken your pain away
He was with you all along
I'll see you again someday!

Diamonds in the Rough

This Journey

I go to sleep with a heavy heart
And then I dream of you
I haven't seen you for awhile
You seem happy and peaceful too!

It feels good to see you in my dreams
Your voice I love to hear
And when you look into my eyes
You see they're full of tears!

No one grieves for you now
In the way that I do
And no one saw your sufferings
In just the way that I knew!

My heart is grieving so much for you
Sometimes it just takes my breath away
I just try to ride the waves,
Each and everyday!

I love to see you at peace in my dreams
To give you a hug once more
And to just hold you in my arms
The way I did before!

Grieving for you had been a journey
And I don't know when it'll end
But I don't walk it alone
For God has been here since it began!

Diamonds in the Rough

The Job You Loved

When you joined the Fire Department
I was so proud of you
You talked about it since you were little
It's what you wanted to do!

When you were a boy you were so excited
When you'd see a rescue truck go by
You wanted to join the academy
Being a firefighter, you wanted to try!

You joined the company when you got older
You worked hard without a doubt
It was your job to help others
Compassion was what it was about!

You once saved a man's life
And he was so thankful to you
From the skills that you learned
You knew exactly what to do!

You enjoyed helping others
You gave the company seven years
You got to follow your dream
You'd still be doing it if you were here!

I miss you talking about your job
And I miss that you've gone away
But I know I'll see you again, son
I look forward to that day!

Diamonds in the Rough

Not In A Million Years

I never thought in a million years
That I'd be telling you goodbye
This is so hard to get through
I can't believe that you died!

I can't even say that word out loud
It just hurts so bad
I just really felt sorry for you
Because of the life you could've had!

I always saw the pain in your eyes
But you didn't think I did
Because of the anxiety and depression
Your suffering, I knew you hid!

I questioned you many times
But you wouldn't be honest with me
I knew you were hiding your pain
So sad it was to me!

I know there are so many people
That suffer with this today
I wish someone could help them
Just take their pain away!

I know that you've been set free now
And I know that you're at peace
The Lord took you home with Him
And your pain, He finally erased!

Diamonds in the Rough

Pain From Loving You

My body and soul are aching
And there's pain in my mind
I just think about you all the time
Some peace I'm trying to find!

The day you left me, my body went numb
And the tears welled up in my eyes
I was devastated and in shock
And I've tried my hardest to get by!

The words I heard that morning
Caused me to feel fear
Sitting there in disbelief
Words a parent should never hear!

I have some of your things in my closet
And your ashes are there too
Wish I could have a moment
To say some words to you!

A year's gone by and I'm still hurting
The numbness has worn off too
It's really just sinking in
That the pain is from loving you!

Diamonds in the Rough

If I Could Reach To Heaven

If I could reach to Heaven
And bring you back again
Just to stay for a while
I think my heart would start to mend!

I miss you so very much
My heart doesn't know what to do
The tears keep flowing from my eyes
Everytime I think of you!

I know the reason that you left
And I couldn't make you stay
I know your mind was troubled
On that day that you passed away!

I just wish you had come to me
And told me what you were going through
I would've tried to understand
And gotten you some help too!

Well, it's all over now
And you're finally set free
I know your home in Heaven
Is the place I want to be!

Diamonds in the Rough

You'll Be In My Heart

It's been a year and I still cry
Because you're not here with me
I know the Angels took you home
That night of the tragedy!

It broke my heart when you left
Because you didn't say goodbye
A note that said you love me
Sometimes I ask myself why!

I know the sufferings that you had
Were so bad you had to go
I wish you could have told me
Because I really didn't know!

I don't know how long this pain will last
But it's just broken my heart
I take it one day at a time
I'm sad because we're apart!

I know one day my heart will heal
And the tears will dry up too
But it's just so hard for me right now
Because I'm missing you!

You were my boy, my only son
And oh, how I adored you
A good heart, compassionate
And very handsome too!

Diamonds in the Rough

I'll long for you the rest of my life
You'll be in my heart to stay
I know the Lord will get me through
And I'll be with you one day!

Diamonds in the Rough

To All The Mothers

To all the mothers that have lost a daughter or son
And today they can't be here
Your heart is aching inside you
And your eyes are welling up with tears!

You've never missed someone so much
As you miss them on this Mother's Day
You wish things could be different
And that they could've stayed!

They'd walk through that door on your special day
And your heart would jump for joy!
It was enough to just see them
You're missing your girl or boy!

There couldn't be a better gift
Than to hear them say, I love you!
You're thinking back to those times
Just know God's getting you through!

He sees the sadness in your heart
And how you long for your child to be here
They'll never pay you a visit again
So, you're just longing to feel them near!

Just remember the special times you had together
That no one can take away
Those memories are nestled in your heart
And it's where they will stay!

Diamonds in the Rough

So, I just want to say Happy Mother's Day
I'll be thinking about you today
And that the Lord will be with you
And He'll wipe your tears away!

Diamonds in the Rough

Stormy Storms

My life has been a journey
I've seen sunshine and I've seen rain
Difficulties that wouldn't go away
Tragedies that brought me pain!

Although I always knew the Lord
Was looking down on me
Ready to come to my rescue
And then to set me free!

He must think I'm strong
To give me what I've gone through
I never had to tell Him my struggles
My sufferings He already knew!

He comes here with arms wide open
And He sits a while with me
His Holy Presence comes over me
Then peaceful I can be!

I wanted to give up at different times
I couldn't see God that clear
Even though He didn't feel close
He was always here!

God must have a good reason
For taking care of me
Here when I couldn't feel Him
He'd bring me through the Stormy Seas!

Diamonds in the Rough

I owe the Lord my life
Because He gave His life for me
I'll never be able to pay Him back
Maybe in Eternity!

Diamonds in the Rough

Through My Tragedies

Lord, you know me so well
My sufferings and trials
Sometimes you don't answer me right away
But I know you will in a while!

You always know what's best for me
And you have my best interest at heart
When I cry out to
You I have much peace that you've brought!

I really don't understand your ways
They're not for me to know
I trust you with all my heart
And someday the answer,
You'll show!

You've seen all the struggles and pain
That have come my way
And you've been here through all of them
Each and everyday!

I'll never be able to thank you
For all you've done for me
But, I know you'll be satisfied
With being my Father through Eternity!

Diamonds in the Rough

My Longing To Help Others

The Lord has let me live this long
To accomplish His plans for me
I haven't always known what they are
But I think now, I can see!

I have a longing to help others
I can see the pain in their eyes
I know their heart is broken into
I want to help them get by!

So many people suffer alone
They have no one to turn to
I really feel so bad for them
Wish it was something I could do!

I count on God to get me through
He comes to me when I'm alone
He knows me inside and out
My struggles He's always known!

So many are out there suffering
If they would just turn to Him
God loves them so much
He hasn't changed, He's still the same!

Diamonds in the Rough

God can use the gift He's given me
To maybe help people cope
And to tell them that
He's there to give them hope!

Diamonds in the Rough

I Trust In Him

Although I'm upset about my son
And many days I still have tears
I really don't know if I could make it
If I didn't have the Lord here!

I don't know how people make it
If they don't call on Him
He wants to get them through
Before their light goes dim!

Sometimes it's maybe hard to trust God
I've had that problem before
And then I started having faith in Him
I feel closer to Him then before!

He has just truly blessed me
I just can't thank God enough
And He never leaves me
When things get really tough!

It doesn't matter what I've done
He's always there to forgive me
I can't believe how much He loves me
His child, He wants me to be!

I will never stop trusting the Lord
No matter what comes my way
I'll always lean on Him
He gets me through each day!

Diamonds in the Rough

He Sets Me Free

Son, I loved you to the moon and back
And I miss you even more
I can't wait until I see you again
To see what God has instore!

A home in Heaven, hard to imagine
That someday I'll be there too
After my work is finished here
Once again I'll be with you!

It might seem like a lifetime
But, Eternity is forever
We're just here a short time
Then we'll be together forever!

Thinking these thoughts, calm my soul
It's what helps me get through
Knowing there's a place like Heaven
And having a Father that loves me too!

He knows all of our troubles
He watches us as we sleep
Always there to pick us up
When the pain gets too deep!

God is watching and waiting
With us He wants to be
To invite us to His Heavenly home
And then to set us free!

Diamonds in the Rough

Life's Trials And Tribulations

Life has trials and tribulations
We're not immune to them
If you will draw close to God
Then your strength will come from Him!

The Holy Spirit came to me last night
I felt a peace like I've never known
My heart felt calming and tranquil
I know He'll never leave me alone!

Our heart and mind are sometimes fragile
When heartache comes our way
We go to God and plead with Him
To get us through another day!

The Lord has never left my side
He does what He says He'll do
When I'm down and brokenhearted
His love will see me through!

He is my great Redeemer
A true friend in time of need
Just trust Him in the race of life
And He'll always take the lead!

Diamonds in the Rough

His Love For Me

I am a fighter, I will survive
No matter what come my way
The Lord is my refuge and strength
He's with me everyday!

I don't know what I'd do without Him
He always has a listening ear
Although others will let me down
He is always here!

Although I've never doubted Him
Because I know He's in control
Still this pain is crushing
It hurts down in my soul!

God's ways are not ours
And I know we don't understand
Even though He might feel far away
Just know He holds us in His hands!

I've drawn closer to Him
Because He's here for me
Even though it's been a trying time
His love still sets me free!

Diamonds in the Rough

He'll Wipe My Tears Away

I had someone talk about my grief
They said I should be moving on
They didn't understand our bond
I've loved you since the day you were born!

All the days you've been gone
Has strengthen my love for you
The ones that haven't lost a child
Really don't have a clue!

My body feels like it's weighted down
This feels like it many stones
It feels like it will never end
When I'm grieving I feel so alone!

I love to see you in my dreams
I wake up happy the next day
You're so excited talking about Heaven
You always have a lot to say!

I know I can't be with you right now
But I'm looking forward to that day
When I'll see you and Jesus there
And He'll wipe my tears away!

Diamonds in the Rough

Heaven Bound

I knew you must have been Heaven bound
When you disappeared that night
You had left and were missing
You were nowhere in sight!

I really felt the worse had happened
And when I was told that day
I just couldn't believe my ears
When he said you'd passed away!

My heart just jumped out of my chest
As I tried to keep it together
But it hit me that moment
That you'd be gone from this life forever!

I know for sure I'll see you again
So that gives me some hope
But losing you is so painful
Sometimes it's hard to cope!

I know you didn't want to hurt us
But there was no way out
You fought this illness for so many years
You were ready to go without a doubt!

I don't blame you for leaving
Because I know what you went through
I look forward to being with you
And I love and miss you too!

Diamonds in the Rough

You'll Abide In Him

I guess my love wasn't enough
To wipe your tears away
But, I don't blame you for leaving
I know you couldn't stay!

Fighting this illness day after day
Although you call on God for relief
You might have felt it was too late
But you stuck to your belief!

I wish I'd known how much you were suffering
Although it would have broken my heart in two!
Things would maybe be different
I could've gotten some help for you!

I know you don't want to come back
And leave your Heavenly home
No more pain and tears
You're just so free to roam!

And your favorite thing to do there
Is sitting by Jesus's side
Singing and praising Him
In Him, you'll always abide!

Diamonds in the Rough

It Doesn't Feel Real

Losing you has been so painful
I've felt like I couldn't get through
The Lord has been right beside me
To help as I grieve for you!

It just doesn't feel real to me
That you won't be back to stay
I haven't stopped thinking of you
Since that day you went away!

Most people that haven't had this loss
Don't really have a clue
They don't know what to say anymore
They think our grief should be through!

We don't expect them to understand
Because they've never lost a child
Since this grief is so painful
It's going to take us awhile!

I've prepared myself for this suffering
Maybe later I can let this pain go
I wish I could have figured it out
There were things I didn't know!

I hope in the years to come
Maybe this grief will be done
Someday we'll meet again
I love and miss you son!

Diamonds in the Rough

Grief So Painful

I know you're crying your eyes out
This pain is bearing down on you
And you're really tired of fighting
You just want it to be through!

I know that feeling, oh so well
I've cried a million tears
My heart and mind have been shattered
Because my son isn't here!

The Lord looks down and He sees me
He sees the pain that I bear
And when it gets pretty bad
I go to Him in prayer!

Sometimes I don't feel Him as much
But I still know He's here
I ask Him to watch over my son
And let me feel he's near!

I know I will get through this
I've climbed high mountains before
God's going to make something beautiful out of this
I'm anxious to know what He's got in store!

I hope I can help others
Because I know what they're going through
Some people have no one
So it's the least I can do!

Diamonds in the Rough

He's Bottling Up Our Tears

My son looked like he was asleep
When I bend over to kiss him goodbye
It was the hardest thing I had to do
Is be strong when I needed to cry!

I should have let the tears just flow
Because my heart was crying out
It was to be expected
This is the worst pain, no doubt!

I've lost a close loved one before
My husband has been gone awhile
But the grief doesn't compare
To the pain when you lose your child!

Of course, I grieved for my husband
And it took awhile to heal
But this is different some how
This grief for my son, feels so real!

I know I'll be missing my son more
As the years go by
The grief will maybe let up some
But there'll still be tears in my eyes!

I owe God for all my strength
He's the one that gets me through
He bottles up all your tears
And He wants to be there for you!

Diamonds in the Rough

At Peace I'll Be

This grief has been hard on me
I just need to rest for a while
Although God is getting me through
I'm tired of this tribulation and trial!

I've never had anything last this long
I've been crying over a year
I just thought the pain would be gone by now
I just want to feel my son near!

Sometimes I can't catch my breath
Because a big wave is here
When it hits so powerful
Then comes the anxiety and fear!

I cry out to God, and He's here
A peacefulness comes over me
I know it's only from Him
Such relief it will be!

This grieving can be so lonely
Even when people are around
Sometimes I'm by myself
And my crying is the only sound!

It's just so gut wrenching
My body is feeling the pain
Pain like I've never known
I feel like I'm going insane!

Diamonds in the Rough

I'm not going to give up this fight
Because God is pulling for me
He knows that I am strong enough
One day at peace, I'll be!

Diamonds in the Rough

Our Grief Washed Away

Someday God will call me home
Oh, what a Glorious day!
I'll be with my family
And they'll have a lot to say!

We'll talk about everything under the sun
And see what God has instore
It'll be a place like we've never known
And our suffering will be gone forevermore!

Our grieving here can't compare
To the glory we will see
All our worries and anxieties
Will be gone for you and me!

What a beautiful life we'll have
We'll be young and never old
Just spending time with Jesus
And our children we will hold!

Thinking about this helps a little
And I can't wait until that day
When all our grief is gone
And God will wipe our tears away!

Diamonds in the Rough

Heaven Is Where They Belong

There are people that are so lonely
And they're brokenhearted inside
They're just trying to get through their grief
Because their child has died!

It's the hardest thing you'll ever do
Is telling your child goodbye
I did it and it broke my heart
But I never asked God why?

He knows everything about us
And our children too
He know about the grief you have
And He wants to get you through!

He knew our children were suffering
So, He took them home with Him
Now they know His love and peace
And He's taking care of them!

So, we don't have to worry now
They're not in pain anymore
When the Angels led them to Heaven
And they walked right through that door!

Now they're there with Jesus
And singing the most beautiful songs
All the Angels are gathered around them
There in Heaven where they belong!

Diamonds in the Rough

A Sign

I haven't seen a sign from my son
Some see cardinals and feathers
Although I know I'll see him again
Where we'll be in Heaven forever!

Maybe I won't get a sign
That tells me, he is here
I just long to hold him
And feel that he is near!

I miss my son so very much
These feelings are hard to control
I know I won't be seeing him soon
But I keep him in my heart and soul!

I remember when he was a little boy
He always wanted to please me
He worked with me, planting flowers
So happy he would make me!

He always had a compassionate side
And he was sentimental too
I loved him more than life
And I wonder if he knew!

I'll never forget my precious son
He was the apple of my eye
And the last time I saw him
I leaned over and kissed him goodbye!

Diamonds in the Rough

We Need Compassion

We don't have feelings that are just like others
Our emotions are all our own
Some know what we're going through
But this grief feels so alone!

I feel guilty when I cry
Because two years have gone by
Some thinking I should be done grieving
That I shouldn't have tears in my eyes!

The truth is they can't feel our pain
They just don't have a clue
They've never lost a child before
Don't know what we've been through!

I wouldn't wish this pain on anyone
It just hurts to the core
Some people just can't accept it
They can't take anymore!

Even with the Lord beside me
There's still a hole in my heart
It might stay there for a long time
Pain and heartache it's brought!

So, if you see me crying someday
Just think about what I've gone through
A little compassion goes a long way
Be glad it hasn't happened to you!

Diamonds in the Rough

You're On My Mind

I'm just sitting here with you on my mind
Knowing that I'll get along
It's so hard to grasp what happened
But I know that I am strong!

The Lord gets me through this time
But there's still pain in my heart
It's just that it's part of grieving
Because my son and I are apart!

It gave me a broken heart when you left
And my heart is still broken today
I didn't know when you left last time
That you'd be going away!

I want to watch videos of you
When you were just a boy
I loved you being my son
You brought me a much joy!

But I know if I watch them
Tears will be running down my face
But, then I'll have to remind myself
That you're in a better place!

I'm sorry you had to leave so soon
And I truly understand
That you wanted to be at peace
And have God hold you in His hands!

Diamonds in the Rough

Mother's Day

For a lot of mothers, this Mother's Day
It's a day that can be real sad
Their eyes swell up with tears
Thinking about the children they had!

Whether it's been months or years
You're really missing your daughter or son
You'd do anything to have them back
You knew them when they first begun!

You picture them walking in with flowers
And a kiss on your cheek they'd give
Happy Mother's day and a big hug
You just long for them to have lived!

Last Mother's Day was my first one without my son
And this one will be just as sad
You never forget your babies
I think about the good times we had!

And there are little babies that didn't make it
And your pain is just as real
Knowing you couldn't see them grow up
A broken heart, you feel!

So, to all the grieving Mothers out there
I will say a prayer
And maybe you will feel better
And your pain won't be as hard to bear!

Diamonds in the Rough

The Grief That Stays

A few friends don't call anymore
Since I lost my son
I guess they think I should be finished
With this grief, I should be done!

Well, it really doesn't work like that
It just doesn't go away
Grief comes to me uninvited
And in my heart it stays!

Someday when the time is right
These eyes may not shed anymore tears
But I've been told not to count on it
This grief could last a few years!

It's the hardest pain my body's felt
And I don't see it moving on
How can you live with a broken heart
I've loved him since the day he was born!

I watched him grow from a child to a man
He was a precious son to me
I never thought I'd lose him
Lord please come and set my heart free!

There are things I wanted to talk with him about
But the time never felt right
He had so much going on in his mind
Which led up to that tragic night!

Diamonds in the Rough

The Lord has got my back on this
He really is my best friend
Don't know what I'd do without Him
In Him, I can always depend!

Diamonds in the Rough

A New Life

I'm listening to sad music
There's tears running down my face
Although it should be comforting
Because it talks about a Heavenly place!

I know that you are there now
And your tears have been wiped away
It's just so hard to get through this
I think about you everyday!

I can't imagine your life now
What an amazing sight
Walking through Heaven with the Lord
And He's finally made everything right!

I know you have happiness
There's love and peace for you
Your dad anticipated your arrival
He was waiting for you too!

Now you and him have bonded
Like you never had before
All your pain and tears are gone
You won't suffer anymore!

I can't wait to reunite with both of you
What a Glorious day that will be
You'll meet me at those pearly gates
A new life there will be for me!

Diamonds in the Rough

God Was There For You

I taught you when you were a little boy
All about Gods love
And about the blessings
He gives He watches us from above!

Your illness started when you were so young
I thought it was so unfair
For a child to go through this
Your pain was hard to bear!

I did everything that I knew of
To help bring you along
I hated what this was doing to you
It just felt so wrong!

I prayed for you, your whole life
I just wanted the best for you
I just couldn't see you suffering
But I knew God would bring you through!

This illness got the best of you
I sadly watched you over the years
I really felt so helpless
I saw your pain and tears!

I wish you'd had a better life
Your suffering just broke me into
But, now I don't have to worry
Because one day I'll be with you!

Diamonds in the Rough

I Have Hope

Times of trouble come to us
Trials and tribulations we see
So difficult to get through them
Sometimes humble we'll be!

I've climbed many mountains in life
Getting to the top was tough
I felt I wouldn't make it
I knew I'd had enough!

God's there to pick me back up
He's not going to let me fall
Although sometimes it gets pretty bad
And I feel I'm against a wall!

I trust the Lord to give me strength
I don't know if I can go another day
So He pulls me through this
He then takes the pain away!

It's so comforting to have God with me
He never leaves my side
Sometimes I pull away from Him
And He knows that I haven't tried!

This grief will last my lifetime
But God will help me cope
If I didn't have Him in my life
I wouldn't have any hope!

Diamonds in the Rough

So, I will try to keep it together
It's all that I can do
Someday I will see you again Son,
I miss and love you!

Diamonds in the Rough

Poems For You

I've written alot of poems for you, son
I feel like it helps me get through
This pain in my mind is agony
Because of my love for you!

I can't control feelings in my heart
They come to me left and right
I try with all my might
They torture me day and night!

Yesterday I had a really bad day
I just couldn't stop the tears
You were constantly on my mind
I can't believe it's been a year!

A year of pain, so heartbreaking
I've never had this before
A pain that runs so very deep
I feel I can't take any more

But the Lord tells me that I am strong
Because of the life I've been through
He knows what I'm dealing with
I'm grieving hard for you!

I thought it would go away after time
But it is worse than ever
I can't wait to see you again
And then we can be together!

Diamonds in the Rough

God Gave You Rest

I know you didn't physically suffer
On that night you passed away
But you had to be in great anguish
You dealt with it night and day!

I'm so sorry that I couldn't help you
The way that I wanted to
You were stubborn in your ways!
This illness was killing you!

You never told me that you needed help
But deep down I knew
How you suffered year after year
And you just couldn't get through!

I know you asked the Lord for help
But He knew what was best
He watched you and was saddened
So He decided to give you rest!

Even though my heart is broken
I feel a little relief
I know you're there in Heaven
And this I surely believe!

I will hold you in my heart
Until my days are through
I look so forward to seeing you
I love and miss you too!

Diamonds in the Rough

I'll Hold You In Heaven

Lord, you lead me through still waters
When there's a storm raging in me
I don't feel that I can make it
But above the storm, you can see!

You can calm this storm in an instant
Bring peace into my heart
For my son, I'm hurting
Because I don't want you to be apart!

These waves are crashing over me
The most powerful ones I've found
They come to me unexpected
And shove me to the ground!

I try to keep my eyes on you,
Lord You know how painful this has been
You're the only one that can lead me through this
In you, I'll always depend!

I'm getting through this grief, the best I can
Although I feel so alone
It's just bearing down on me
It feels my body is filled with stones!

It's hard not having any control
Over the feelings I have inside
Just coming at the oddest times
I've fought this pain, I've tried!

Diamonds in the Rough

My mind and body are crying out
This pain runs to the core
I talk to the Lord above
And tell Him, I can't take it anymore!

I can feel the relief He brings me
A peacefulness in my soul
I long to see you in Heaven
And your precious body, I'll hold!

Diamonds in the Rough

Sometimes I Just Breathe

Sometimes all I can do is breathe
I open my mouth but can't cry
The pain is so gut wrenching
I pray for the Lord to get me by!

I stay locked away in my room most times
I really don't get out much
I just long to see my sons face
And I need to feel His touch!

Most times I do this alone
This grief that I despise
It comes at me with such force
Tears are pouring out of my eyes!

I just want to lay down on the floor
Kick and scream and cry!
Just get this out of my system
So I don't feel like I will die!

I don't plan on giving up yet
There are things I want to do
I have my daughter and grandchildren
And I want to write these poems for you!

I want to be able to comfort someone
And feel deep inside their soul
I wish that I was able
To give them back, what life has stole!

Diamonds in the Rough

God Answered Our Prayers

These days there's a storm raging in me
And other times the sun shines so bright
My mind just goes back to you
I'm dwelling on that tragic night!

You needed me but I wasn't there
But the Lord heard your cry
You pleaded with Him to take you home
There was nothing else you could try!

You were so tired of your life
It was spinning out of control
In your heart, you'd given up
You felt great pain down in your soul!

You didn't want to hurt anyone
You just wanted it to be over fast
I saw you suffer all your life
I knew that you wouldn't last!

I prayed to God to lead your life
The way He wanted it to go
He saw in your heart, great anguish
This, I didn't want to know!

I tried to pretend the pain wasn't there
That it wasn't so real
Sometimes you appeared to be happy
But I knew your mind would never heal!

Diamonds in the Rough

Now I know you're with the Lord
God finally answered our prayers
He took you home and wiped your tears
And one day I'll be there!

Diamonds in the Rough

He Wiped Your Tears Away

I wish I had said, I love you!
The last time you were here
I only hugged you and said goodbye
Now I'm shedding many tears!

You never knew how dear you were
And the love I had for you
Was enough to cover a lifetime
And maybe Eternity too!

A year now has come and gone
Where does the time go?
My bleeding heart is still living
I can't believe how I miss you so!

I saw the tears in your eyes
And the pain you tried to hide
I knew there was nothing I could have done
I just thought about you and cried!

There were things I wanted to say to you
I knew your mind wasn't well
You often tried to ignore me
But I could always tell!

So now you're free of pain for good
I wish I could've been there that day
The moment you walked into Heaven
And God wiped your tears away!

Diamonds in the Rough

His Strength

I need to get you off my mind
Just for a little while
I'm just sinking deeper and deeper
Because I miss you, my child!

You had your whole life ahead of you
But you just couldn't live that way
Your mind wasn't well, you were suffering
Each and everyday!

I use to pray for God to help you
I didn't know the plans He had
He knew how much you struggled
And I'm sure that made Him sad!

I really feel burdened with this pain
I didn't know it could get this rough
The Lord hears me when I pray
I tell Him that I've had enough!

He's walking me through this grieving time
He knows how much I can take
Even though I feel like giving up
God knows that I won't break!

He gives me His strength to make it through
And I have a little bit of my own
It's just the times when the pain is bearing down on me
Is the time I feel so alone!

Diamonds in the Rough

I know this too shall one day pass
But I have a long way to go
I can't wait to see you again
I love and miss you so!

Diamonds in the Rough

Peace He Brings Me

I can't believe I've been in such pain
I feel like I'm sailing stormy seas
The waves are rushing in, so powerful
They're crashing down on me!

I don't want to feel this agony anymore
It's devastating to my soul
Although it could get better
In my heart right now is a hole!

A hole that will never be filled
Only memories I'll hold of you
Sometimes I'm at my witts end
I just don't know what to do!

I pray for strength everyday
I know God hears my plea
Just when I think I can't take it anymore
He then comes through for me!

There's a cost for those we love
I never thought I'd feel
A devastating loss for you
A pain in me that's so real!

I don't have to do this journey alone
The Lord is here for me
I've called on Him time after time
Peaceful He wants me to be!

Diamonds in the Rough

A Better Place

I didn't have to walk in your shoes
To know what you were going through
This illness was just a dead end
I saw what it did to you!

I have walked the same path
Through the pain and tears
Sometimes wanting to give up
Because it lasted for so many years!

It was so sad to see you suffer
I wish I could've taken your place
To see you happy and at peace
And all your pain erased!

You hid your pain from me most times
But sometimes I could see through you
I watched you as you went downhill
When you gave up too!

There wasn't a way for me to help you
So, I just felt so sad
I hate that you had to suffer
From this illness that you had!

I've suffered a lot too
But God is getting me through
It's been such a hard time for me
And I know you suffered too!

Diamonds in the Rough

I'm feeling happy where you are now
I just want to see your face
I love and miss you so much
But you're in a better place!

Diamonds in the Rough

The Very Best

I wake up early some mornings
And I thank God for the day
He has truly blessed me
Even though you've gone away!

He sees the tears that I cry
The emptiness in my soul
I just want to see you again
Your body I just want to hold!

The Lord has been a tremendous help
He's getting me through each day
I go to Him in tears, sometimes
And ask Him why you couldn't stay!

Although the answer, I already know
You had a better plan
A plan to bring him home to you
Now you hold him in Your hands!

This had been a rough journey
That you've brought me through
I don't know if I could make it
If I didn't depend on You!

The bible says, when I'm heavy burdened
You will give me rest
You are a loving Father to me
You give me the very best!

Diamonds in the Rough

I Miss My Husband

Oh, how I miss my husband
He's been gone for years
I ask God to heal him
I prayed to Him in tears!

I wasn't sure how I'd make it
With two children to take care of
We still really needed him
He showed us so much love!

I've never wanted anyone else
You're still my husband to me
Even though I can't see you
In my heart is where you'll be!

You were a good family man
I was blessed when God gave me you
And He blessed us with children
Now we have grandchildren too!

I tell your grandson about you
And he'd like to meet you someday
I tell him you're now in Heaven
And that is where you'll stay!

I look forward to seeing you again
And our precious son
God will bring me there one day
When my life down here is done!

Diamonds in the Rough

In A Better Place

I have all of your hats and some clothes
That I'm going to hang on to
When I bring them out years from now
My heart will still be missing you!

Your son is growing up so fast
He is so much like you
I'm proud to call him my grandson
He's so sweet and compassionate too!

I know he'll have questions
He'll want to ask me someday
Like what happened to you
Why you had to go away!

I know you're at peace now
And I hope he'll be too
He has his life ahead of him
And I know He'll be missing you!

He won't understand until he's older
Why you had to leave so soon
You didn't mean to hurt him
But you mind suffered a deep wound!

I try not to let my grandson see
Tears running down my face
I'll try to help him understand
That you're in a better place!

Diamonds in the Rough

God's Purpose For You

Your time on this Earth was shortened
I wish I'd had some way to know
The pain you were going through
As you planned a way to go!

I know you wouldn't hurt me
But there was no end in sight
You were tired of suffering
You just gave up the fight!

I wonder what God's purpose was
For you being born
You struggled all your life
And left me here to morn!

I've never questioned God, not once
Since you've been gone
I know He's got you in His arms
You're in Heaven where you belong!

As much as I'd like to have you back
As bad as my heart aches for you
I know God's wiped away your tears
And He's given you love and peace too!

Diamonds in the Rough

My Heart Is Sad

When my heart is feeling really sad
And I've fought it with all my might
That's where God comes in
And helps me win this fight!

It's not going to be easy
But alone I don't have to be
He is there to help out
Although I just can't see!

There's no light at the end of the tunnel
It will be dark for a while
Because I've been so traumatized
I've lost my precious child!

The worst pain I've ever felt
Because I loved him so much
It's really taking a toll on me
I just want to feel his touch!

It could be a long time until I see him
But, I'm waiting for that day
When I can put my arms around him
We'll have so much to say!

I know this blow will soften
As my heart starts to mend
I thank God for His help
Down this long road He's been!

Diamonds in the Rough

I Grieve For You

I never thought in a million years
That this grief would come to me
Sorrow has taken over
And peaceful I can't be!

I never thought I'd lose a child
The way that I lost you
The person I was has faded away
My life has changed, it's true!

I never thought I'd be alone
And grieve the way I do
Even when others are around
I'm still grieving for you!

I know people mean well
But my pain they can not feel
It's going to take a long time
Before my heart will heal!

I take this one day at a time
That's all that I can do
Although it may get better
I'll always grieve for you!

Diamonds in the Rough

My Heart Will Mend

Memories are flashing through my mind
Memories I have of you
Everyday seems to get worse
But God helps get me through!

I have faith and I trust Him
He always knows what's best
I call on the Lord when I'm in pain
And I feel His peace and rest!

He will walk through the fire with us
This is His promise to me
He's been here all along
But sometimes it's hard to see!

When I feel burdened with this sorrow
And I have a heavy heart
I go to the Lord and feel better
Love and peace He's brought!

I know this suffering will last awhile
I don't feel it going away
But God walks through this trial with me
And I know He'll always stay!

I'm trying to imagine Heaven
Where I will see you again
What a peaceful place
 And my heart will surely mend!

Diamonds in the Rough

Mother's Day

Today is Mother's Day for some
Those who've lost their daughters and sons
It's bringing sadness to my heart
When will this pain be done!

My son didn't let me know
The pain he was going through
I just found out too late
All along he knew!

He knew that he was ready to go
But I had no clue
The amount of suffering he was in
I never knew what to do!

If I could just turn back the clock
And have him here with me
Maybe he could seek help
More peaceful he could be!

He didn't know the answer
To the suffering he went through
I prayed to God to help him
But in His wisdom He knew!

He knew it would be better for
Him to take my son home
He watched the pain in his life for many years
And he lived his life alone!

Diamonds in the Rough

I know for sure that he's at peace
I wouldn't want it any other way
I really don't understand
But God will show me the answer someday!

Diamonds in the Rough

I'll Keep You In My Heart

I'll always have a place in my heart
And I'll always feel you there
Just waiting for the day
When this pain I can bear!

I have pictures of you all around
And sometimes they make me cry
Just to know that you are gone
I hated to tell you goodbye!

Your ashes are in my closet
And your dads sit there too
You wanted them spread together
So I'll do this for you!

I wasn't ready when it happened
It was too overwhelming for me
To let go of the only thing I have
I know so sad I would be!

You left a life so young
I hated to see you part
But just know I'll always love you
I keep you in my heart!

This has happened for a reason
That only the Lord knows about
But I know you're safely in His arms
And this I have no doubt!

Diamonds in the Rough

Remembering You

I've been through all the holidays now
Since you were last here
I was saddened by your absence
And my eyes were full of tears!

It just doesn't feel real to me
Even though I know it's true
That you've been gone for a year
And I'm really missing you!

I try to keep myself busy at times
I'm going to have a garden this year
Last summer I let it go
I was heartbroken because you weren't here!

You use to help me plant flowers
When you were a little boy
I watched you work in the dirt
You brought me so much joy!

You were such a blessing
That the Lord gave to me
Now He has taken you home
In my heart you'll be!

I wouldn't call you back for anything
Because you're finally at peace
I have many memories of you
My love for you will never cease!

Diamonds in the Rough

I'm Thinking About You

I sat on the bench that's by your tree
And I talked to you for a while
Tears start rolling down my face
The Lord has allowed this trial!

Some days it seems much easier
Other days the grief overpowers me
I know this will go on for awhile
Still brokenhearted I will be!

I think back to the day it happened
I can't get it out of my mind
I just picture you lying there
Some peace I need to find!

I ask the Lord to release this pain
Just so it will help me get through
I know there are stages of grief
I have to go through while I'm grieving for you!

I know you had to be in great anguish
You were walking the streets that night
Trying to make a decision
So alone. no one in sight!

The detective came up the next morning
He told me what you had done
I couldn't believe what I was hearing
I'd lost you, my only son!

Diamonds in the Rough

I know this pain will one day lessen
And my tears will dry up too
But for now you're on my mind
I'm so busy thinking about you!

Diamonds in the Rough

Thinking About You

The tears in my eyes have returned to me
For a few weeks I haven't cried
It's really hitting me full force
Thinking about the way they you died!

My heart just screams without you
I'm trying my best to get through
The waves of pain are crippling
Every time I think of you!

I know you're better off where you are
There are no pain or tears
And I know that your heart was aching
When you lived your life down here!

It's just that it hurts so much
Since you've been gone away
You didn't know the pain I'd be in
I've been crying since that day!

I cry out to God to give me relief
To just soften the blow
Because it's getting pretty tough
How long it will last, I don't know!

I know there will come a time
When my heart will slowly mend
And I know that God gets me through
On Him I always depend!

Diamonds in the Rough

There With Jesus

Someday at our home in Heaven
God will wipe our tears away
He'll reunite us with the ones we love
Oh what a Glorious day!

No more pain or heartache
Only a future and a hope
But for now we endure
God's here to help us cope!

In your short life you've been through alot
The Lord is looking down on you
He wants you to tell others
How you're making it through!

Without Him life would be harder
More than you and I know
Because that we don't know to worry
Because He loves us so!

You'll never forget your mother
Her sweet and kind ways
That made you the person you are
And you'll see her again one day!

Diamonds in the Rough

But for now just know she's with Jesus
She's there watching over you
She's walking streets of gold
Where the Heavenly skies are blue!

Donna Carpenter for Julie Salmon In Memory Of Lee Salmon June 21st 2015

Diamonds in the Rough

Heaven

Heaven must be beautiful son
Because you are there
Just hanging out with Jesus
Without a worry or care!

It will be so wonderful
A place that I've dreamed about
A real paradise for you and me
Somedays I'll be on me way no doubt!

I'll spend Eternity with the Lord
And I'll be free to roam
Beautiful sights everywhere
Yes, this is my Heavenly home!

I know down here there's work to do
The Lord does count on me
To spread His love to everyone
So joyful they will be!

Heaven is real and God prepared it
It seems to good to be true
A place without pain or tears
He created it for me and you!

Diamonds in the Rough

He's Wiped Your Tears Away

Before you closed your eyes at night
I had already said a prayer
For God to keep you safe and sound
I longed for you to stay around!

I saw you go downhill so fast
You just wouldn't let me in
So much pain and sadness
Depressed you'd always been!

I wanted a way to help you
I tried throughout the years
I felt so much sorrow for you

And I fought my own pain and tears!
Maybe there was more I could have done
To help you on your way I watched you as you struggled
Each and everyday!

Only God knew your heart
He knew what you were going through
Maybe you couldn't understand
How powerful His love was for you!

I'll see you again, my son
Oh what a wonderful day
I know you're there with the Lord
And He's wiped your tears away!

Diamonds in the Rough

Trust The Lord

In this life that we live
You take the good with the bad
No matter how hard
And no matter how sad!

When pain and suffering come to you
Remember who's in control
He reaches down to comfort us
Deep into our soul!

I feel like I've grown closer to the Lord
Even through this tragedy
He's allowed it for a reason
He promises to be here for me!

At times it's difficult to trust Him
We just don't understand
Don't understand God's ways
But know He has us in His hands!

The Lord says our tears aren't in vain
He sees each one that falls
And when we're doubting an answer
His peace He gives us all!

It takes a lot of strength to courage
To hold our head high
God will one day explain everything
Once in Heaven we'll know why!

Diamonds in the Rough

Your Heart's Door

You may not believe that God is
Because of the pain in your heart
Not knowing why He allowed it
So, you'd rather stay far apart!

I had doubts and questions
It seemed like God wasn't there
When in fact it's just the opposite
The Lord is everywhere!

Before He can heal your pain
You have to let Him in
There's no reason to blame Him
Because of this world of sin!

He came and did His part
Now He's waiting for you
He wants to open doors
And heal all your heartheartache too!

Don't be afraid, give Him a chance
I did this years ago
Finding out how much He loved me
I just couldn't let Him go!

Now is the time to trust Him
What have you got to lose?
You're looking for a way out
And God is the best news!

Diamonds in the Rough

Heavenly Birthday

Son, you left a year ago
And on your birthday too
They say time heals all wounds
Why am I shedding so many tears for you?

I just wanted to say goodbye
And just hug you so tight
I'm really here missing you
I'm fighting it with all my might!

I just want to open my eyes
And see a smile on your face
There with God so peaceful
And all your pain erased!

Sometimes I wish that Heaven would open
And God would call me home
So I can be with you once again
And we'd never be alone!

I don't feel that will happen
For I have work on this Earth to do
Being a servant for Jesus
And taking care of my family too!

Diamonds in the Rough

We celebrated both of your birthdays
As we stood around your tree
Each one letting a balloon go
This time was special to me!

Donna Carpenter Travis' First Birthday In Heaven And His Earthly Birthday April 6th 2020

Diamonds in the Rough

He's All You've Got

God sees your hurt,
He feels your pain
He sees tears coming down like the fallen rain!

He says, "Reach out to me
He says, "Take my hand
I see what you're going through
And I know you don't understand!"

"Your ways are not my ways
And it's very hard to see
How a just and loving God
Can allow such tragedy!"

"I know in your heart there an emptiness
Your soul is crying out
This life is so confusing
Not knowing what it's all about!"

"I have the answer, please let me show you
Will you open your heart and mind?
I promise I will never let you down
And I'm the best friend you'll ever find!"

"My love and strength are always here
Though the trials and tribulations be alot
And you'll never know that I'm all you need
Until I'm all you've got!"

Diamonds in the Rough

"I too lost my only Son
When He died upon that tree
Even if you'd been the only one
I would've sacrificed Him to set you free!"

I'm asking you to trust Me now
You're searching and I'm the cure
I'll bring you through the raging storms
And safely to the shore!"

Diamonds in the Rough

Refuge From The Storm

"Although the crashing waves come down on you
And the raging storm takes form
Be Still And Know That I Am God,
Take refuge from the storm!"

"I'll carry you as I promised
My arms reach out, take hold
I'm the One you can turn to
I'll heal the misery in your soul!"

"I know the plans I have for you
I'll reveal them at My will
I long to richly bless you child
Just be patient now, be still!"

"Don't be burdened with unanswered prayer
You'll someday know my plan
But for now rest assured
That I hold you in my hands!"

"I see you when your heart cries out
I hear your desperate plea
When you think you can't sink any lower
Then I'm here, just turn to me!"

"Trials and tribulations come and go
But I am always here
I see your pain and anguish
I carry you, though you're unaware!"

Diamonds in the Rough

"Trust in me with all your heart
And I will give you peace
Although the difficult times will come
My love will never cease!"

Diamonds in the Rough

Promised Land

You came to me in a dream last night
In perfect peace, pain free
It's the dream I've been waiting for
And it brought much comfort to me!

My son said, "This place is so amazing
More than I ever dreamed it would be
I know you can't comprehend
All there is to see!"

"The best thing is I'm here with the Lord
He's so mesmerizing to me
And I finally understand
How His love has set me free!"

"In Heaven with Him for Eternity
No heartache, no pain, no tears
I can't wait for you to see
It's so wonderful here!"

He said, "Mom, you go on with your life
I've just gone before you
I'm safe in my Fathers hands
And one day you'll be too!"

"I know this is so hard for you
And I know that you don't understand
But there is so much waiting for you
When you get here to the Promised Land!"

Diamonds in the Rough

God's There

I know you're sitting there brokenhearted
Because of all you've been through
Once again give your life to God
You'll be surprised at what He can do!

He doesn't want us to suffer
Like we do with the pain and tears
He wants us to depend on Him
And He wants to feel us near!

You life may seem out of control
Your mind, your soul, your heart
But if you draw close to God
You'll never feel apart!

He really wants the best for you
Although you might not understand
That when He feels far away
He holds you in His hands!

Your problems and pain God knows about
Never doubt His love
A love that conquers everything
From our Heavenly Father above!

Be still and know that He is God
Go to Him in prayer
Trust Him with your life ahead
Your tribulations He'll help you bear!

Diamonds in the Rough

You're At Peace

I'll never forget you my son
And when you were a little boy
I cherish the memories I have of you
You brought me so much joy!

There was a caring side you had
You really had a good heart
If I could just have you a little longer
We wouldn't have to be apart!

I watched you as you got older
Some things seemed to trouble you
As you tried to hold it in
Deep in my heart I knew!

You struggled hard and I saw
I saw you fight everyday
I know in your heart you prayed
For the Lord to take you away!

I saw you fight your battles
And it really broke my heart
I knew you couldn't stay here
You knew it was time to depart!

I haven't held it against you
Because I knew you were seeking peace
I'll treasure your life forever
And my love will never cease!

Diamonds in the Rough

A Special Grandson

I'm staring at your memorial tree
And thinking a lot about you
My little grandson is making a garden nearby
He has much work to do!

He doesn't talk about his dad that much
He doesn't want to upset me
He's such a good and compassionate boy
An awesome man he will be!

I watch him as he works so hard
He's so much like my son
I am so proud of him
Now I think the garden is done!

My grandson won't let me pay him
He just wants to do things for me
I'm so happy to have him
He'll always be special to me!

I love to teach Him stories
From the Bible long time ago
I taught his dad these stories too
Every Sunday to church we would go!

I'm glad I have my grandson
A beautiful gift from my son
He is so important in my life
My heart I think he's won!

Diamonds in the Rough

Can't Compare

The sufferings we have can never compare
To Heaven, God's made for us
It belongs to us all
If in Him we put our trust!

Sometimes the pain doesn't move
It seems it's here to stay
But if we go to God in prayer
He promises He'll make a way!

I've lost you and I'm in great pain
It seems to be lasting forever
Although I know that it can't last
Because we'll one day be in Heaven together!

It's hard to comprehend a place
Where there's no heartache, pain or tears
It seems to good to be true
To see our loved ones that we hold dear!

I'm trying to focus on that
Through this storm in the downpour of rain
I go to my Father and ask
If He'll walk with me through this journey of pain!

So far the Lord is getting me through
I never thought in a million years
That I'd be walking this path
And crying this many tears!

Diamonds in the Rough

I'm trying to focus on my son
I know he's where he should be
I'm trying to picture the smile on his face
Someday soon I will see!

Diamonds in the Rough

A Journey

Life is but a short journey
Compared to Eternity
Our suffering aren't to be compared
To the happiness there will be!

Time has gone by so fast
Since God called you home
I can't wait to be with you
All through Heaven we will roam!

I try to concentrate on that
Instead of the sorrow I'm in
It could only be a short time
When in Heaven my heart will mend!

The Lord has His arms around me
Bringing me comfort each day
As I absorb His goodness
I know He's the only way!

He must think I'm strong
To give me what I'm going through
I never thought in a million years
My heart would ache this much for you!

I look forward to going home
It's hard to imagine that day
There with our Lord forever
And to be healed in every way!

Diamonds in the Rough

Save Me A Place

I feel my heart's so heavy
Gentle tears roll down my face
How long will it be now
Before I get to a different place!

I'm trying so hard to be strong
But it hasn't gotten me anywhere
This grief comes uninvited
Much pain, so hard to bear!

If Heaven would just open for a moment
And I could see your face
I would see the peace you hold
Because you're in a Heavenly place!

You were my first and only son
Sent to me from the Lord above
So much joy you brought
And you taught me how to love!

I knew you couldn't stay any longer
And I wouldn't have asked you to
I knew all along you had given up
But there was nothing that I could do!

As you're enjoying your Heavenly home
Please save a place for me
I could be there real soon
With you where I want to be!

Diamonds in the Rough

Don't Cry For Me

I dreamt of my son the other night
It was the best dream I've ever had
He approached me with a smile on his face
He said, "Mom, don't look so sad,

I'm in my Heavenly Home now
It's where I've longed to be
You know I'm happy and without pain
So please don't cry anymore tears for me!"

"You didn't know the dept of my suffering
I managed to hide it from you
I'm thankful that you tried to help
You did the best you could do!"

"The pain and heartache are no more
God's taken me under His wing
Surrounded by His glory
And listening to the Angels sing!"

"I can't wait for you to be here
It's such an amazing place
I was mesmerized when I met my Savior
When I looked upon His face!"

"Surrounded by His glory
As I knelt down before His throne
At that moment I knew
That I would never be alone!"

Diamonds in the Rough

"Someday God will call you home
And you will kneel before our King
Every pain and tear will be wiped away
And you'll feel the peace and love He brings!"

Diamonds in the Rough

Always Strong

I've cried many tears in my life
And God has bottled up each one
He's seen me at my lowest point
To Him I wanted to run!

There were times I didn't feel this way
I doubted Gods love for me
Over the years I came to see
That He wanted to be a Father to me!

It took awhile for me to trust Him
To find out if He was real
I went to Him with a sincere heart
And my wounds He started to heal!

God said that He'd been here all this time
And He's watched me for so long
There have been times when I doubted His strength
But now in Him, I'm always strong!

The Lord has been so good to me
In Him I can always depend
When I go through tragedies
He is here to help my heart mend!

I can't wait to meet my Heavenly Father
He has done so much for me
I want to show Him that I'm thankful
And I'll do that through Eternity!

Diamonds in the Rough

I've Moved Ahead

In the race of life, I've moved ahead
Only because God has gotten me through
If I didn't have Him by my side
I don't know what I would do!

God says He won't put too much on me
He must think that I am tough
There have been times when I questioned Him
When this grief has gotten to be too much!

So, God has gotten me through this
And I know Gods words are true
Every time I have a doubt
I remember that He loves me too!

The poem about the footprints
There was only one set in the sand
That means that God carried me
He had me in His hands!

Sometimes God allows suffering
Because it will make His plan work out
He wants us to trust Him
He knows things we know nothing about!

When I get to Heaven I'll surely know
What plans God had for me
I will finally understand
What in this life I just couldn't see!

Diamonds in the Rough

Don't Tell Me

Please don't tell me to just move on
When you don't know my pain
It feels like a storm inside of me
And then comes the downpour of rain!

Don't tell me it's been a long time
And that I shouldn't be crying
Well the truth is my heart's not healing
Sometimes I feel like I'm dying!

You might think that I'm not strong
But I know that not to be true
I have fought this with all my might
I pray it never happens to you!

It's been a very long journey
My soul is crying out
Wondering how I'll get through
I sure know what grieving is about!

Your heart really feels like it's broken
The pain just won't go away
The days and nights are the same
I pray that I'll heal someday!

Diamonds in the Rough

You're Healed

Today I'm feeling kind of down
Inside my heart is sad
Thinking about the memories I have
Of all the fun times we had!

I try not to focus on tomorrow
But rather getting through today
God is here when I need Him
He will provide a way!

When I saw you last
I thought you'd be around for awhile
I think about your personality
And how you made me smile!

From the beginning I loved you
You were my special boy
Your whole life I adored you
I felt so much joy!

I look forward to seeing you
My love for you is so much
I know now that you're alright
You're healed by the Masters touch!

Diamonds in the Rough

I Want You Near

Time has really flown by this year
And oh, how I miss you so much
I just want to hold you tight
I long to feel your touch!

I have a blanket I cuddle with
Made out of clothes you had
I hold it close to my heart
The tears come and I'm feeling sad!

I want so much to have you near
To see you in my dreams
Right now you feel so far away
A million miles it seems!

I have no doubt that you're at peace
I wish I could feel it too
But for now I'll carry on
And one day reunite with you!

I know your life had a purpose
And I know God had a plan
I don't know now, what is was
But I know He holds you in His hands!

I thank the Lord for sharing your life
You brought me so much joy
My love for you will never cease
You'll always be my sweet boy!

Diamonds in the Rough

Never Ending Peace

When you were just a little boy
And you grew into a man
I asked the Lord to keep you safe
To hold you in His hands!

I taught you about His mercy and grace
And I told you about His love
If you should have a problem
Call out to the Lord above!

I know you talked to Him sometimes
And I know you said your prayers
When you were facing hard times
And it felt too much to bear!

God is our friend in time of need
Our great Redeemer too
I saw Him as you struggled
Reach out His hands to you!

He tried to pull you through the stormy seas
And over the capsizing waves
He told you to be still and know
He's God Stand tall and strong, be brave!

This life just got the best of you
But you didn't go down without a fight
I watched you as you fought so hard
Until the Lord called you home that night!

Diamonds in the Rough

I know if I could see you now
You'd be walking streets of gold
Strolling along with your dad
Never ending peace down in your soul!

Diamonds in the Rough

Your Time To Go

I touched your lifeless body
As I leaned over and kissed you goodbye
It really felt like a bad dream
I didn't know you were going to die!

They wouldn't let me visit to long
Your hand I just wanted to hold
I couldn't believe it was you lying there
I loved you with my heart and soul!

It just doesn't feel real to me
That you had to leave this way
It's just broken my heart
I cry almost everyday!

I know the pain will lessen one day
So that's what they tell me
I can't see it happening
Heartache is all I can see!

He was my only son so young
I felt this would happen one day
I tried to put it out of my mind
But the feeling wouldn't go away!

Maybe I could have tried harder
My son I wanted to save
I really did the best I could
And lots of love I gave!

Diamonds in the Rough

I feel like this terrible illness won
I watched it year after year
Sucking the life out of him
Now my son isn't here!

I know now he's peaceful
It was his time to go
Until we meet again
I love and miss him so!

Diamonds in the Rough

At Home With Jesus

I know you're not in pain now son
The Lord has taken that away
He's given you a new life there
And it's where you'll forever stay!

I used to pray for you each day
And ask God to get you through
He knew of your pain and suffering
And He knew you were unhappy too!

I know He tried to help you
Because it was out of your control
Fighting those horrors in your mind
Hurting way down in your soul!

I don't blame you for leaving
It's all that you could do
You fought so hard to conquer it
And you prayed to the Lord too!

He knew you'd be at peace with Him
So He let you go
Even though you left us
We still love you so!

Diamonds in the Rough

No Pain Or Tears

I'm thinking about you and the times we had
When you were just a boy
I was so thankful to have you
You were my pride and joy!

I taught you many things about life
But the most important one
Is that God loves you so much
Trust Him with your heart, my son!

He's there for us in time of need
He sees the tears we cry
Not expecting us to go it alone
He's there to get us by!

The things I taught you, you understood
But questioned why God allowed your pain
He wants us to depend on Him
He's there in the sunshine and the rain!

God saw you struggle throughout your life
And He reached His hand down to you
He told you He longed to bring you peace
And His love for you is true!

The suffering in your mind is healed
No more pain or tears
Just forever with the Lord
Your Savior that holds you dear!

Diamonds in the Rough

As much as I miss you
I'm glad He holds you in His hands
And maybe it won't be too long
Before we can be together again!

Diamonds in the Rough

In The Promised Land

I don't think it is selfish
That I decided it was my time to go
So much pain and misery
I was in Most people didn't even know!

Years and years of emptiness
Knowing something wasn't right
These moods and monsters in my head
I fought with all my might!

I may have look fine on the outside
And even given you a smile or two
But so much anguish on the inside
I just didn't know what to do!

It was a fight from the very beginning
A problem that wouldn't go away
As the days turned into night
I pleaded with my myself to stay!

I never wanted to hurt anyone
Because of what I've done
I left a loving family
And a precious son!

I hope when he's older
You'll help him understand
That I loved him but just couldn't stay
Now I'm in the Promised Land!

Diamonds in the Rough

A Heavy Heart

My heart is so heavy right now
It's almost been a year
The fog and numbness are gone
It's sinking in that you're not here!

I feel like I will explode
This is everyday
So hard to hold it in
I just wanted you to stay!

I would've traded places with you
I long for Heaven too
It's just so very sad
You had so much living to do!

When the anniversary of your passing comes
In just a little while
It will also be your birthday
We'll celebrate you, my child!

We'll release a few balloons
And read a poem too
It will be a day of tears
We'll say we love and miss you!

Maybe as the years go by
My grieving for you might be done
I'm not sure I can believe that
I love you so much, my son!

Diamonds in the Rough

Imagine Heaven

I'm trying to imagine Heaven
It'll be a place of perfect peace
Just hanging out with Jesus
All pain and heartache will cease!

It's how to imagine a place like this
I've known about Heaven all along
Since I was a little girl
There were bible verses and songs!

The bible speaks about Heaven
So many beautiful things there
Mansions with jewels, streets of gold
There without a worry or care!

Crystal rivers and mountains so tall
From the tree of life we'll eat
Just being there with family
And many others we want to meet!

I want to talk to Mary, Jesus's mother
Ask what it was like to carry a boy king
It must have been a real privilege
And to feel the joy God brings!

God has promised us His paradise
And it's waiting for you and I
Someday we'll finally arrive
And we'll tell this life goodbye!

Diamonds in the Rough

Hard Times

I've seen hard times come and go
And I know it's made me stronger
And sometimes the pain is so bad
I wonder if I can take it any longer!

I ask God to help me through
I can't do it on my own
He comes and stays by my side
He'll never leave you alone!

I've always felt closer to Him
When tragedy comes my way
I call out to Him and He hears my plea
And that's how I get through each day!

Life is but a journey
Sometimes the mountains are steep
I've climbed a lot in my life
I just call out to God and weep!

He says He'll bring something good out of this
Although it may not seem that way
He has it all planned out
Down to the very day!

Don't know why things happen like this
We just can't understand
But if we trust in God
He'll hold us in His hands!

Diamonds in the Rough

You Longed For Heaven

You've been on my mind a lot today
I just wish I could see your face
I know you're pain free and peaceful
Because you're in a better place!

The reality of your death is sinking in
I didn't know it could get this bad
I've been relying on God to get me through
But still I'm feeling sad!

Been crying all day long
So scared I'll lose control
All the fog and numbness are gone
My heart is aching down in my soul!

I wish you could've had a better life
Wish it was something I could've done
I just longed to see you happy
I loved you so much, my son!

I know you're with the Lord now
And that just amazes me
My mind can't comprehend
Such a place where you longed to be!

So, you just rest there so peaceful
And someday I'll be there with you
Thank God for His eternal gift
And hug your dad too!

Diamonds in the Rough

I'll See You, Son

So sorry son that I wasn't there
On that terrible and tragic night
I know you had great anguish
And you fought it with all your might!

I saw the sadness in your eyes
So often throughout the years
I know God heard your desperate plea
To rid you of your pain and tears!

I didn't know you'd be Heaven bound
At the age you were, so young
The Lord knew all this time
Before your life had begun!

I never questioned God for taking you
From me and our family
I knew in my heart you were ready
Heaven is where you wanted to be!

I've never ask God to bring you back
Because this life just wasn't for you
I'm sorry you had so much suffering
But I know God helped you through!

My memories of you will never fade
We had special moments, some fun
I'll cherish them the rest of my life
And I'll see you again, my son!

Diamonds in the Rough

Waves Of Pain

This anguish I feel is overwhelming
Your body I just want to hold
If I had just had the chance to tell you goodbye
It would have lessened the pain in my soul!

These daggers of grief are piercing my heart
Yet I've never asked God why
I already know the answer
But still these tears I cry!

I fear one day, I'll lose control
Not being able to hold on
I feel like a piece of my life is gone
You were my boy, my firstborn!

This pain I'm feeling is heartbreaking
I long to bid it farewell
To push it away through the capsizing waves
I only wish I knew how!

These waves rush in to conquer me
I try my best to stand tall
But even though I feel that I'm strong
The powerful ones make me fall!

I have no choice but to give it my all
A fighter I've always been
I'll always love you my son
And I know I'll see you once again!

Diamonds in the Rough

I Am Thankful

Many days and months have passed
And I'm still broken inside
Sometimes it's to hard to handle
With all my might I've tried!

I call out to you, Lord Jesus
And I know you hear my plea
Please come and be by my side
Please come and rescue me!

I've called out to you time after time
And I know you're always there
You lift me up and give me strength
This pain you help me bear!

Feelings inside like I've never felt
Just trying to get by, to cope
I can feel your presence right now
You want to give me a future and hope!

I'm thankful to you for all you've done
I couldn't never find a better friend
Here for me, my strength and shield
In you I can always depend!

I will praise you till the very end
What my time on Earth is done
I will shower you with Thanksgiving
For giving me your only Son!

Diamonds in the Rough

If You Could See Me

Mom, "If you could see me now
Those tears you cry would dry
Even though my body is gone
I really didn't die!"

"When I floated up towards Heaven,
I saw the most brilliant light
And then two beautiful Angels
Were ready to show me the sights!"

"They carried me through the gates of Heaven
I've never seen such a place
Then I caught a glimpse of Him
And I looked upon His face!"

"I knew right away it was Jesus
Wearing a pristine robe so white
There is no sun in Heaven
He is the only Light!"

"I looked into His eyes so peaceful
It just took my breath away
I could feel the love He had for me
I really didn't know what to say!"

Jesus said, " Welcome home, my child
I've been waiting for you
Welcome into Heaven
I'll give you a body brand new!"

Diamonds in the Rough

I then knelt down in front of Him
I was mesmerized by His beauty
He said, "I've wiped your tears away
And with me you'll always be!"

"You see mom I'm happy and at such peace
Heaven is more than I thought
I can't wait to see you again
And I love you with all my heart!"

Diamonds in the Rough

A Changed Life

You wonder what this life is for
Sometimes it seems so bad
Pain and tears, no reason to live
Your life has been real sad!

No peace, joy, or happiness
Has ever come your way
You just want out of here
Not caring the time or day!

Some people wander their whole life
Just trying to figure it out
No light at the end of the tunnel
God's help is something they doubt!

You're locked inside your own little world
Not letting anyone come in
They wouldn't understand your place
Couldn't know the road where you've been!

I once felt this pain and heartache
That ripped my soul in two
This life didn't seem worth living
I had much pain like you!

After many years I found a reason
A reason that turned my life around
It wasn't fame or fortune
Jesus's love I'd finally found!

Diamonds in the Rough

He showed me His love is sincere
He knew the path I'd been through
He told me to go tell others
That the same He can do for you!

Diamonds in the Rough

You've Gone Before Me

If I could just walk through Heaven
And be with my family
I'd never want to come back
Because it's where I want to be!

Someday when the Lord calls me home
And I finally get to see
All of my loved ones that are there
They'll open up their arms to hug me!

I know you've gone before me
And how I miss you so much
The day God called you home, son
You were healed by the Master's touch!

I feel peaceful at knowing that
But my heart still aches for you
Sometimes the pain seems unbearable
So many tears rolling down too!

It's almost been a year now
Time is flying by so fast
I still can't believe that you are gone
I remember the day I saw you last!

We were talking about your birthday
And little did I know
That God would be taking you home
Because He loves you!

Diamonds in the Rough

Hard Roads

I've been down a lot of hard roads in my life
Since I was just a girl
So I know God gives me strength
To make it in this world!

Losing my son has been the hardest
A pain that I've never known
A wave so big it takes my breath
In this grief I feel all alone!

Didn't know it was going to last this long
It's hard to fight these feelings anymore
I don't know what the future holds
Only God knows what's in store!

I know He has a plan for me
I just don't know what it's about
I need to take one day at a time
And trust Him without a doubt!

In the past I had some questions
About all that I've been through
I needed to have an answer
An answer that only God knew!

I haven't questioned the Lord about my son
Because all things work together
And I will see him again someday
And so thrilled we'll be there forever!

Diamonds in the Rough

A Smile Upon Your Face

I'm feeling really sad today
You've been on my mind so much
I'm just missing you more than ever
I just want to feel your touch!

Sometimes I picture you smiling
And I can tell you're pain free
What an awesome place you're at
I'll bet you're watching over me!

I don't know how long this grief will last
And I must not hurry it along
I'm just taking it one day at a time
God's given the ability to be strong!

Thoughts keep running through my mind
About the life you had down here
You couldn't live it to the fullest
Because of the anxiety and fear!

I really tried my hardest
But I guess it wasn't enough
It was just out of my hands
I know at times it was tough!

God's got you in His hands now
I couldn't ask for a better place
Can't wait to be with you again
And see that smile upon your face!

Diamonds in the Rough

I'll Take This Pain Away

This awful disease of depression
Is not something that's in your head
When it hits hard, it's crippling
You can barely get out of bed!

Most people don't understand
Because they haven't walked in our shoes
But let me tell you something
It's not just sadness or the blues!

Anxiety and fear grip your mind
You think you're going to die
Pain and racing in your head
I cry out to God and ask why?!

I tell Him that I hate this disease He's allowed
I don't feel like it will ever cease
And then one day He spoke to me
He said, "I want to bring you peace!"

"I've watched you suffer for many years
I see the misery in your soul
Someday when you're here with me
The answer to you will be told!

For now just know I'm with you
Every step of everyday
My plans for you aren't finished
Someday I'll take your pain away!

Diamonds in the Rough

No Pain In Heaven

I know your heart was broken
When you got the news that day
You were in shock and disbelief
That he had to go this way!

Just a young man with a future
It is such a shame
How he was taken so violently
Someone else is to blame!

I'm sure he had plans for his life
A good career, a family he could have had
But that's been taken away
And this makes me so sad!

The guilty one is out there
I hope they find Him one day
And throw the book at him
Just take him far away!

I know he was the apple of his mother's eye
And she'll cherish him forever
She truly adored her son
And she's looking forward to them being together!

No pain or fear where he's at
Just experiencing Gods love
All his tears are wiped away
There in Heaven above!

Diamonds in the Rough

Trusting You

He didn't see her coming
Around the curve that night
Going way to fast
What a horrible looking sight!

Only seventeen, her life's now gone
What are her parents to do?
Such an awful heartache
But they're giving their pain to you!

You said, "Come to Me when you're heavy burdened,
And I will give you rest"
They've read it many times before
Wondering if this is a test!

Her parents have so much trust in the Lord
They never even questioned His plan
They know that all things work together for good
When you're there in His loving hands!

This tragedy has brought them sorrow
They feel their heart's been broken in two
God's there with them when they're hurting
And they know they can always trust You!

The days and months have quickly gone by
And they're missing their little girl
In Heaven they'll be reunited
Her home is not of this world!

Diamonds in the Rough

They'll never know the answers
Until they see their daughter someday
For now they're just trusting in God
When in Heaven, He'll wipe their tears away!

Diamonds in the Rough

Through The Storm

"You come to me in pieces
A heart that's so much in pain
Don't wait until the storm is over
But learn to dance in the rain!"

"Through the storm I'm with you
Every step of the way
Please don't ever doubt Me
I'm here with you to stay!"

"Many times you've called on me
And those times I've heard you cry
I will walk through the fire with you
And help you to get by!"

"I've suffered more than you have child,
My hands, my feet, my side
They beat me and spit in my face,
Because of your sins, I died!"

"Many times I've heard you cry
Wishing you would come to me,
You were so absorbed in your sorrow,
With your heart, you could not see!"

"I've seen your courage through this all"
Your soul and spirit are strong,
I promise when you get to Heaven
It will be where you belong!"

Diamonds in the Rough

Many Moods

The many moods that invade my mind
My life passes by me now
The dark, black dog of depression
I long to bid you farewell!

I long to be free of the raging storms
That carry my mind out to sea
Stranded in the capsizing waves
Lord please rescue me!

Rescue me from the anxiety and fear
That chisel away at my soul
From the fierce daggers that pierce my heart
This monster is out of control!

Sometimes this black dog lies dormant
But that's few and far between
Then it's back to terrorize me
So cold, so ugly, so mean!

When the upside of you comes crashing down
And the light in your mind goes dim
That's when Gods strength is made perfect
Reach out and take hold of Him!

We forget sometimes God's stronger than it
This disease that can destroy a mind
Don't try to face it all alone
He's the best source of help you'll find!

Diamonds in the Rough

My Journey

I've seen bad days come and go
And I didn't think I could hold it together
So much suffering and pain
Feeling like it will last forever!

I know who I can depend on
And I know who will get me through
Giving me His strength and love
He can do the same for you!

I feel a wall slowly coming towards me
I'm pushing it with all my might
It's so strong and powerful
But I can't give up this fight!

I've fought many fights in my life
And this one is lasting awhile
It feels like my body is weighted down with stones
I'm tired of this tribulation and trial!

The Lord is helping me get through this
But there's only so much I can bear
I really feel His strength in me
When I go to Him in prayer!

I know one day this pain will lessen
And my heart will start healing too
But right now I have to go through this journey
It's all that I can do!

Diamonds in the Rough

Come To Him

You think you're at the end of your rope
Feeling like you can't go any longer
Pain and heartache set in
Only the Lord can help you get stronger!

He wants you to count on Him
He's the One that can get you through
A lot of times He's helped me
So I know He can help you too!

God hates to see you hurt
He sees each tear you cry
He sees how hard you're trying
Just to get yourself by!

Those tears you cry aren't in vain
He bottles up each one
He's longing for you to come to Him
To offer you Jesus, His Son!

We live in a fallen world
But still God is here
He loves you more than you can imagine
And to Him you are so dear!

Please, will you give Him a chance
Because your life is upside down
He will never forsake you
He will turn your life around!

Diamonds in the Rough

I've known many heartaches
And God has never abandoned me
He wants you to come to Him
So peaceful you will be!

Diamonds in the Rough

Suicide

Suicide robs you of your life
May it be young or old
It is no respect of persons
It eats away at your soul!

You feel like you don't have a life
You don't want to live anymore
Nothing changes over time
Then comes depression once more!

It eats away in your mind
You know your had enough
You try to fight it with all your might
But it's strong and really tough!

Sometimes there are voices
Then the anxiety sets in
You really don't know where to turn
No one knows where you've been!

You describe it as horror
What it's putting you through
You're really ready to just give up
You're thinking about doing it to

So you sit back and make the plans
But you don't want to hurt anyone
Thinking how bad they'll miss you
You are a father and a son!

Diamonds in the Rough

Your family gets the phone call
They say that you are gone
You were so tire of fighting
You really weren't that strong!

Diamonds in the Rough

Jesus Suffered Too

If I could just touch the hem of your robe
I know I would be set free
You are the great Physician
I know peace you'll bring to me!

I'd like to look inside Jesus's eyes
Soft and gentle they would be
Then talking to Him for hours
Heaven is what I want to see!

My family are having the time of their life
Just being there with you
It's much more than they imagined
And you've wipe their tears away too!

God knows all our heartaches
He has suffered too
He lost His only Son
He died for me and you!

Knowing he inherited this disease from me
Makes me feel real bad
Alot of time he was real troubled
Alot of times he was sad!

If you know someone out there
That has this illness too
Don't allow them to be silent
Tell them they can talk to you!

Diamonds in the Rough

So many people are hurting
They don't know where to turn
Just be there for them
Show them your concern!

I know my son has found peace now
And God's wiped his tears away
I can't wait to be with him
Oh what a Glorious day!

Diamonds in the Rough

If I Could

If I could just hold you one more time
And look into your eyes
I'd see that you are trying to tell me
That it's time to say goodbye!

If I could meet you on the other shore
It wouldn't matter how long it would take
Because of my love for you son
If do anything for your sake!

If we could just talk awhile
There are things I want to say
Like how much you mean to me
And that I prayed for you each day!

If I could see the crown you're wearing
And a robe as white as snow
I would see you talking to Jesus
He'd be telling you how He loves you so!

If I could just see the peace in your heart
If I could look upon your face
I would see so much happiness
Heaven is an awesome place!

Someday I will see these things
And the tears in my eyes will dry too
No more pain or fear
Just spending Eternity with you!

Diamonds in the Rough

God Chose You

If I could just get a glimpse of you
My heart would just leap for joy
To see you without pain and tears
You'll always be my precious boy!

The Lord chose you to be my son
And I had you for alittle while
You were so special to me
And you always made me smile!

God had a reason for taking you
Maybe it was your time to go
I wasn't ready to lose you
Because I loved you so!

I try to imagine what you're doing
I know you and your dad are together
I can't wait for the day to come
When we'll be there forever!

Many memories I have of you
They're nestled safely in my heart
That's where I will keep them
So much happiness to me you brought!

Diamonds in the Rough

God's Plans

Some people are bitter at the Lord
Because of all they've gone through
He doesn't need to take the blame
Because He is not punishing you!

There are bad things in this world
That God's always known about
He is a good, fair God
And this I have no doubt!

There are things in this world that are unfair
But God didn't plan it that way
He gave man a chance from the beginning
In the garden He wanted them to stay!

I've questioned Him over the years
But I never thought He was to blame
Someday He'll explain it to us
Why He's allowed such pain!

I go to the Lord in ernest prayer
When things aren't working out
I really don't understand His ways
It's hard to figure out what life's about!

I know that God's been good to me
No matter what's come my way
I don't know what His plans are
But I will know someday!

Diamonds in the Rough

Someday I'll Know

When storms come in my life
I try to focus on the One that can get me through
I cry out to God in misery
It's the only thing I can do!

I think of all the pain I've had
That's happened throughout the years
When I call out to God
He wipes away my tears!

Only He knows how much I can stand
Through it all He's made me strong
I go to Him with an earnest heart
In prayer with God is where I belong!

I ask Him why so much heartache
What is your plan for me?
The Lord hasn't answered me lately
But someday I will see!

I'll see why He's allowed such suffering
All the suffering I've been through
At times I would drop down to my knees
It was the only thing I could do!

It may not be in my lifetime
But someday I'll understand
As the Lord takes me home
I'll know When I get to that promised land!

Diamonds in the Rough

I Taught You

I use to cover you up at night
I'd say, "Pray to God now, son"
He didn't understand how He worked
How can He answer everyone?

I taught him to have faith in God
He'll be there to work things out
You were then so young
You didn't know what life was about!

When you were older, you turned to the Lord
You told me about it that night
You were excited and happy
You said, "It just feels right!"

One day God answered a prayer
That I'd been praying about
After He came through for you
You trusted Him without a doubt!

I had the opportunity to teach you about Jesus, God's Son
And we learned to be thankful
Because He's done so much for us!

I know we'll be together again
And I wish you didn't have to go One day
I'll understand I miss and love you so!

Diamonds in the Rough

Your Heavenly Birthday

Son, you left a year ago
And on your birthday too
They say, time heals all wounds
Why am I shedding more tears for you?

I just wanted to say goodbye
And hold you, oh so tight
I'm here really missing you
I've fought it with all my might!

I just wanted to open my eyes
And see the smile on your face
There with God, so peaceful
And all your pain erased!

Sometimes I wish Heaven would open
And God would call me home
So, I could be with you once again
And we'd never be alone!

I don't think that will happen
For I have work on this Earth to do
Being a servant for Jesus
And taking care of my family too!

We celebrated both of your birthdays
As we stood around your tree
Each on letting a balloon go
This was so special to me!

Diamonds in the Rough

My Home In Heaven

There will come a day in the future
When my pain will be no more
The Lord will finally call me home
I can't wait to see what He has in store!

All the tragedies in my life
All the pain I've had to endure
When I get to that Glorious place
God will wipe my tears for sure!

Just knowing I have a Heavenly home
Where there's no heartache, pain or fear
Just receiving love from the Lord
And my family that I hold dear!

Just the thought of Heaven
Helps me get through these trials
My husband and son are there together
I might see them in a little while!

When the Lord is ready for me
And my work on Earth is done
To Heaven the Angels will lead me
Through fields of flowers I'll run!

I won't remember about this life
Because it will fade away
I can't wait until that day comes
With my Savior, I'll always stay!

Diamonds in the Rough

People Are Hurting

We're losing so many of children
They leave this world in a terrible way
Sometimes we tend to blame ourselves
Because we couldn't make them stay!

They usually don't let on
To the amount of pain they're in
Not wanting to worry anyone
Down a long road they've been!

Mental illness is to blame
Bad thoughts going on in their mind
At times we don't realize this
Because there really aren't any signs!

Our children just couldn't hang on
The pressure was too much to bear
They really fought it with all their might
Sometimes even saying a prayer!

People have been made to feel ashamed
So that's why they're not reaching out
They're tired and they're weary
Helping them is what it's about!

Please reach out to others
An understanding friend you can be
And say a prayer for them
That God may set them free!

Diamonds in the Rough

The Strength God Gives

These waves of pain just hit me
They're the worst I've ever felt
Knocking me almost to my knees
I have to accept this hand I've been dealt!

Something good will come out of this
But right now I just can't see
I don't know the answers God holds
And I don't know His plans for me!

I'm more than willing to be His vessel
To help someone that's in pain
Someone that's struggling through a storm
And through the downpour of rain!

At times I've felt that it's too much
God must know what this is doing to me
Deep inside I know He does
He's making me what He wants me to be!

I never knew that I could handle this pain
The kind that crushes your heart
But with Gods strength and mine
It keeps me from falling apart!

I know He is here for me
Without Him I couldn't get through
His peace passes all understanding
Mercy and grace, He gives too!

Diamonds in the Rough

My future is in the Lords hands
And whatever may come my way
It won't be something I'll face alone
Because He's with me everyday!

Diamonds in the Rough

You're At Peace

For all the times I've called on God
For all that I've been through
Nothing in the past has affected me
The way it did, when I lost you!

I've had some steep mountains to climb
And at times, I wanted to die
Not thinking that I could make it
But God have me the strength to try!

You were the apple of my eye
I treasured the joy you brought
You were my first and only son
And I loved you with all my heart!

I never held it against you
Because I knew you were ready to go
You were ready to go home to the Lord
To the One that loves you so!

It has been a rough year for me
But I know that God's been here
Here to catch me when I fall
And to wipe away each tear!

I know that you're in perfect peace
And you'll never be alone
Just receiving God's mercy and grace
And feel a love like you've never known!

Diamonds in the Rough

At Peace

You came to me in a dream last night
You were happy as you could be
You told me not to worry
That God had set you free!

I ask Him to release you
Of your pain and tears
I saw that you were just hanging on
And you suffered through the years!

I wasn't able to help you
And that made me very sad
But now I know where you are
You're in Heaven with your dad!

It feels unfair that you had this illness
A normal person you couldn't be
I saw you try with all your might!
There wasn't a light at the tunnel to see!

When I get to where I'm going
I will see your peaceful face
I'll know the Lord has healed you
And you're in a better place!

For now, I'll try to move on
Because you would want me to
And someday we will meet again
And be given a body, brand new!

Diamonds in the Rough

God's Got This

There are times I want to scream and holler
And just get it off my chest
There are other times I'm quiet
Just be calm, I need to rest!

These waves of grief just slam me
Never know when they're coming around
They almost knock me off my feet
I open my mouth to cry, without a sound!

My mind is tired and weary
And my body is feeling it too
Don't know how much I can take
What am I supposed to do?

I know that God has got this
But sometimes I wonder why
That such tragedy has come my way
I don't feel like I'm getting by!

God knows when I am burdened
He knows how much I can stand
I don't mean to doubt Him
I know He has me in His hands!

It's just the pain sometimes gets bad
What are we supposed to do?
We're so scared and frightened
Our hearts are broken in two!

Diamonds in the Rough

I know God won't give me too much
He's gotten me through each trial
With His help, I am strong
I'll be better in a little while!

Diamonds in the Rough

God's Got My Back

God is watching and waiting
For you to call upon Him
To get you through your heartache
Before the light goes dim!

I first called on Him years ago
When the pain was way too much
Through trials and tribulations
He always stays in touch!

Down through the years, God's had my back
Like no one I've ever known
When I'm troubled, He's right there
Never to leave me alone!

He brings me peace every day
No matter if the chips are down
He'll never leave nor forsake me
And He's the best friend I've ever found!

Someday the Lord will explain things to us
And I have some questions in mind
About why He loves me so much
And why He never left me behind!

In Him, I've always put my trust
Even though the heartache and pain
The sun will once again shine
After a stormy rain!

Diamonds in the Rough

Hard Times

I've seen hard times come and go
And I know it's made me stronger
But sometimes, the pain is so bad
I don't know if I can stand it any longer!

I ask God, to help me through
I can't do it on my own
He comes to me, He's by my side
He'll never leave me alone!

I always feel closer to the Lord
When tragedies come my way
I call out to Him and He hears my plea
And that's how I get through each day!

Life is but a journey
Sometimes the mountains are steep
I've climbed quite a few in my life
I just reach out to God, and weep!

He says He'll bring something good out of this
Although it might not seem that way
He has it all planned out
Down to the very day!

Don't know why things happen the way they do
We just can't understand
But if we trust in Jesus
He'll hold us in His hands!

Diamonds in the Rough

At Home With Jesus

I know you're not in pain now, son
The Lord has taken that away
He's given you a new life there
And it where you'll forever stay!

I used to pray for you each day
And asked the Lord to get you through
He knew your pain and suffering
And knew you were unhappy too!

I know He tried to help you
Because it was out of your control
Fighting those horrors in your mind
Hurting way down in your soul!

I don't blame you for leaving
It's all that you could do
You fought so hard to conquer it
And you prayed to the Lord too!

He knew you'd be at peace with Him
So, He let you go
Even though, our hearts are broken
We still love you so!

Diamonds in the Rough

He'll Give You Back To Me

God gave you to me, for a little while
In my womb, He formed you
Before you were born, He knew you
He had your life planned out too!

I didn't know He'd take you so soon
And leave me with a broken heart
I loved you more than life
Much love to me, you brought!

I've known for awhile, that you had to leave
I never questioned, why?
I know that you're in Heaven now
But I never got to say, goodbye!

I saw you illness bring you down
You never opened up to me
Most times, you were sad
But now, happy you can be!

God had a reason for taking you home
In the beginning, I just couldn't see
I know someday, I'll see you again
And God will give you back to me!

Diamonds in the Rough

I'll See You Again, Son

I'm so sorry son, that I wasn't there
On that terrible, tragic night
There must have been great anguish
And you fought it with all your might!

I saw the sadness in your eyes
So often throughout the years
I know God heard your desperate plea
To rid you of your pain and tears!

I didn't know you'd be Heaven bound
At the age you were, so young
The Lord knew all this time
Before your life had begun!

I've never questioned God for taking you
From me and our family
I've known in my heart you were ready
Heaven is where you longed to be!

I'd never ask God to bring you back
Because this life just wasn't for you
I'm sorry you had so much suffering
But I know the Lord helped you through!

My memories of you will never fade
We had special moments, much fun
I'll cherish them throughout my life
And I'll see you again, my son!

Diamonds in the Rough

I Love You, Son

Each day this grief is harder and harder
It's finally settled in
I asked God when I'll see you
So we can be together again!

It's been almost a year now
Didn't know the pain would last this long
I rely on God to get me through
I'm fighting hard because I'm strong!

These daggers are piercing my heart now
I long to bid them farewell
Capsizing waves are rushing in
I would conquer them, if I knew how!

I ask God again, when I'll see you
He says just wait and see
Maybe not in my lifetime
But in Heaven!, one day I'll be!

I would love to hear your beautiful voice
Singing praises to the Lord
There are lots of things to do there
And of course you'll never be bored!

Gods been with me from the beginning
He helps me as I mourn
I will always love you, son
You were my boy, my firstborn!

Diamonds in the Rough

I Said Goodbye

It's been awhile, but none the less
I'm still feeling really sad
I miss you, oh, so much
And all the times we had!

I have pictures of you on my dresser
And a cap of yours too
Sometimes these feelings just come to me
At times, just out of the blue!

I'm trying to get through this grief
Each hour, of everyday
I call on the Lord so often I know
He's the only way!

I thank God for the time I had him
He brought me joy, at different times
Since he was born
I've had him on my mind!

I know God wants to get me through
He's promised this to me
I lean on Him, everyday
My comforter, He'll always be!

I know in my heart, why you couldn't stay
I don't have to ask God why?
But my heart was really broken that day
When I kissed you, and said, goodbye!

Diamonds in the Rough

The Peace He Brings

I've been asking God for real peace
Peace that I can recognize
The Holy Spirit brought it to me
Last night, before I closed my eyes!

The most peaceful feeing that I've ever known
Came for a little while, over me
I knew right away what it was
The Lord had heard my plea!

The feeling I felt, was wonderful
It felt like the Lord was right here
Telling me to give Him my worries
And also, my pain and tears!

What a privilege it is to go to God
With our earnest prayers
He answers us in His time
And our burdens, He helps us bear!

There's nothing I have done, to deserve the Lord
He's with me everyday
A love bigger than eternity
It just takes my breath away!

Diamonds in the Rough

Our Child

When you've lost a child, so dear
You can't imagine the pain
The pain of a broken heart
Tears coming down like rain!

Don't be scared to speak our child's name
It makes us feel better then
Sometimes just the smallest things
Can help our hearts start to mend!

Christmas time is upon us
And we're feeling rather sad
We miss our child, and have memories
Of all the Christmases we had!

Sometimes we just really need
Just someone to be here
Talking or sitting silently
Don't be afraid of our pain and tears!

My child now, is in my heart It's where
I want him to be
If you have a minute, please remember
To say a prayer for me!

Diamonds in the Rough

Enjoying Heaven

I hope that you're enjoying Heaven
And sitting at Jesus' feet
Getting to really know Him
I can't wait for us to meet!

Is it everything you thought it would be?
Do the Angels really fly?
These things I'll know when I get there
I won't have to ask God, why?

I knew your new home was waiting
For another Angel to sing
And I know you were looking forward
To the love and peace God brings!

You won't be here for Christmas
But I'll have you in my heart
And feel all the memories around me
We won't seem to far apart!

I'm glad you finally made it there
Heavens where you've wanted to be
Talking to Jesus and walking streets of gold
These things, one day, I'll see!

Diamonds in the Rough

Trust God

In this life that we live
We take the good with the bad
No matter how hard it gets
No matter how sad!

When pain and suffering come to you
Just remember who's in control
God reaches down to comfort us
Deep into our soul!

I feel that I've grown closer to God
Even through my tragedy
He allowed it for a reason
He promises to be here for me!

At times it's difficult to trust the Lord
We just don't understand
We don't understand His ways
But know He holds us in His hands!

God says, our tears aren't in vain
He sees each one that falls
And when we're doubting an answer
His peace, He gives us all!

It takes a lot of strength and courage
To hold our heads up high
God will one day explain everything
Once in Heaven, we'll know why!

Diamonds in the Rough

I'll Move On

My heart is an open wound
The pain runs so deep
Somedays, I might be ok
But other days, I weep!

My soul cries out for you each day
How long will the pain be?
I'm trying to handle it the best I can
But it's really got a hold on me!

The morning I learned of your passing
Was the day that my heart broke into
I've never felt pain, that hard
And it was because of my love for you!

I'm missing you so much right now
It's really taking a toll on me
I'm trying so hard to be strong
I just wish your face I could see!

I'll never just get over you
But I'll learn to just move on
And I've never stopped loving you
Since the day that you were born!

Diamonds in the Rough

He's In A Better Place

My son would pick my flowers
When he was just a boy
He'd bring them to me, blooms only
But it still brought me joy!

Sometimes he was peculiar
I couldn't understand his ways
When he was hard to handle
I would go to God and pray!

Sometimes we'd have a picnic
On a beautiful day outside
Then we would play some games
Then he would go and hide!

Sometimes he would have anxiety
When he was only three
I didn't know how to handle him
And it was so sad to me!

When he was a teen, depression set in
And doctors he had to see
I thought it was so unfair
A normal child, he couldn't be!

I wish Heaven would open up
And I could see his face
He suffered alot in his life
Now he's in a peaceful place!

Diamonds in the Rough

Grief Is Love

The deeper the love of our child
The harder our grief will be
Different things trigger our pain
He was so special to me!

The holidays will be harder this year
There'll be an extra chair
When we're gathered together
It will be difficult for me to bear!

I've been thinking about you, alot lately
You're always on my mind
I didn't see this coming
I wasn't aware of any signs!

I ask God to heal you
From the disease that you had
I guess it wasn't His plan
Which makes me really sad!

I know you're at peace right now
Because you needed a way out
I know you're with the Lord
And this, I have no doubt!

Diamonds in the Rough

I Miss You

Before I close my eyes each night
I always think of you
Imagining that you're standing here
With a glorious body, brand new!

God knew you couldn't stay any longer
So He allowed you to go that way
I'm really missing you alot
As much as I did that day!

Time isn't healing this pain
In fact I think its worse!
I loved you more than life itself
You were my only son, my first!

This pain I'm feeling runs oh, so deep
It runs to the core I know
I'll be with you again
And we'll be there forever more!

For now, I count on God to be here
He's never gone away
And someday I'll start healing
I look forward to that day!

Diamonds in the Rough

Faith

Please don't lose faith in God
When bad things happen to you
That's when you should trust Him more
Because He's going to get you through!

This life is full of tribulations
Pain and heartache we feel
We go to the Lord in prayer
Because we know His love is real!

He'll bring us through as He promised
He sees each tear that we cry
He's always there to listen
When we ask Him the question of why?

He doesn't always give us an answer
He says, He'll show us someday
Show us why our tragedy happened
And He'll take our pain away!

God knows about our suffering
He sees you telling your loved one, goodbye
And He hears you asking Him
Why that person had to die?

The Lord has proven Himself to me
No matter the pain I'm in
He's been beside me this whole time
In Him, I can totally depend!

Diamonds in the Rough

He has been so faithful to me
And I long to know Him better
I can't wait to see His face
And be there with Him forever!

Diamonds in the Rough

I'll See You Again

I dreamt I was in Heaven
And I looked all over for you
I was mesmerized at the beauty
And the sky, oh so blue!

I thought I heard you call my name
You said, "Mom I'm over here!"
As I looked around, I found you
And noticed your eyes were full of tears

"Don't be sad, these are happy tears
I'm so glad that you are here
I've been waiting for you
Finally we can be near!"

"I know you can't stay right now
But God will call you home one day
I know your heart is broken
We can't understand His ways"

"I know when God calls you home
The Angels will bring lead you in
So happy that I'll be
That we'll be together again!"

Diamonds in the Rough

He Set Me Free

I watched you as you cried last night
I saw the tears run down your face
I wish that I could come there
And all of your pain, erase!

"I don't want you to cry for me
I know it's hard on you
So many tears you've cried
You don't know what else to do"

"Just know I'm happy and finally at peace
I'm praising the King Of Kings
I have so much to show you
And you'll feel the love that God brings!"

"I'm really here, walking streets of gold
I really wish you could be here
Singing praises to our Savior
Who we love and hold dear!"

"If you could see me now
This is where I want to be
Here with my Heavenly Father
Because He set me free!"

Diamonds in the Rough

A Broken Heart

Tears are slowly rolling down
As this sad music plays
Music to help me get through
Each and everday

I look at your things in my closet
Wish the tears would go away
I'm having trouble doing this
I know one day, I'll be ok

This pain is working overtime
And the Lord is too
If it wasn't for Him, I don't know
What I would really do

Time doesn't make it any easier
It lays heavy on my heart
God's getting me through now
I'll be better, although we're apart

Yes, one day my tears will dry
And this pain in my heart will heal too
I'll pray for healing until then
To get me through losing you!

Diamonds in the Rough

This Illness

I know you had good days and bad times
I saw you happy somedays
But other times, you seemed saddened
Wish I could have taken your pain away

It started when you were a little boy
And it is such a shame
To have the anxiety and the fear
Nobody was to blame

Wish I could've traded places with you
I would've taken your misery
There was nothing I could do
It often saddened me

I asked God, what was the point of your illness?
It lasted, year after year
I knew I could never fix it
You had so much pain and tears!

I'm sorry you had to live this way
There's nothing anyone could have done
I tried to give you a good life
I love you so much, my son!

I don't know why God allows such illnesses
Maybe stronger He wants us to be
Just know God's getting me through
And He's really taking care of me!

Diamonds in the Rough

Your Hearts Door

You may not believe that God is
Because of the pain in your heart
Not knowing why He allowed it
So you just rather stay apart

I had doubts and questions
It seemed that God wasn't there
When infact it's the opposite
He is everywhere!

Before He can heal your pain
You have to let Him in
It's no reason blaming Him
Because of this world of sin

He came and did His part
Now He's waiting for you
He wants to open doors
And heal your heartache too!

Don't be afraid, give Him a chance
I did this years ago
When I found out how much He loved me
I just couldn't let Him go

Now is the time to trust Him
What have you got to lose?
You're looking for a way out
And He is the best news!

Diamonds in the Rough

Your Gift To Me

A picture of you sits on my dresser
A picture of my grandson too
It's just so sweet, I'm mesmerized
At how much he looks like you!

What a precious gift you left me
I'll treasure him all my days
I love to see him in action
And boy, does he have your ways!

The Lord has truly blessed me
He's such a good, good boy
I've really fallen in love with him
And oh. how he's brought me joy!

I'm teaching him things about Jesus
The same way that I taught you
About how He is our Savior
And how He loves us too!

I'll teach him to trust God with all things
Not to try to figure it out
God is the solution to our problems
That's what His love is about

Thank you again, for your gift
I will cherish him forever
And someday when we arrive
We'll all be there together!

Diamonds in the Rough

Because He Lives

Because God lives I can face tomorrow
I can face the pain that's inside of me
And I know He holds my future
No matter what that might be!

His love for me is amazing
It's more than I ever thought
And when the tragedies come to me
I feel Him more in my heart!

God's seen me cry with tears overflowing
And He then reaches down to me
To help me through the sorrow I feel
The heartache I have, He sees!

I can't believe the blessings that God's given
Even when I'm in deep despair
Sometimes I don't recognize them
He's here to help me with the pain I bear!

I can't imagine where I'd be without Him
He comes to me to soften the blow
He's seen this road that I'm going down
And my future He already knows!

I really appreciate Gods love I feel
And His soothing voice I hear
He's gotten me to where I am today
My Heavenly Father that I hold dear!

Diamonds in the Rough

Thank You So Much!

Published by:

LSW Media Group

Charlotte, NC 28210
Phone: 704.649.6358
For book orders or wholesale distribution
Website: www.lswmediagroup.com

Made in the USA
Las Vegas, NV
03 September 2023